Connecticut's Music in the Revolutionary Era

CONNECTICUT BICENTENNIAL SERIES, XXXI

Connecticut's Music in the Revolutionary Era

by **RUTH MACK WILSON** with the assistance of
KATE VAN WINKLE KELLER

The American Revolution Bicentennial Commission of Connecticut

Hartford, Connecticut
1979

ML
200.7
. C8
. W5

ISBN: 0-918676-17-7
Library of Congress Catalog Card Number: 79-57123
Manufactured in the United States of America
All Rights Reserved

FIRST PRINTING

Contents

THE SELECT HARMONY

Preface

THE systematic study of Connecticut's early musical life has not been undertaken until now. In the absence of reliable information, many erroneous assumptions have been drawn, foremost among them the idea that there was little music outside of church before 1800. The Reverend Samuel Peters' fabricated Blue Law against music, printed in his *History of Connecticut* (London, 1781), has enjoyed long and unmerited credence. As Nathan H. Allen, Hartford organist, pointed out in the 1920s, "There is a misconception as to the attitude of our Puritan forefathers towards music in general. It lies in the minds of many that they took the aggressive course towards music they would have taken towards an outbreak of small pox, or an epidemic of any like contagious disease - something promptly to be stamped out." We intend to dispel these tenacious myths by demonstrating that careful research in the kind of sources cited in the Notes will prove the diversity and vitality of Connecticut's music in the Revolutionary Era.

The commission for this book was originally accepted by Kate Van Winkle Keller. She invited me to join the project later. In June of 1978, under press of commitments to the *National Tune Index,* of which she is originator and coauthor, Mrs. Keller asked me to assume full responsibility for the work and to write the manuscript. She graciously put at my disposal files, notes, and indexes of dance and fife manuscripts and of materials relating to her extensive research on popular and military music. She generously lent books and articles from her library and, during the final stages of the project, was able to offer additional time for research assistance. Her indefatigable energies were cheerfully devoted to retrieving whatever information was requested.

Special thanks for their assistance are extended to Librarian Elizabeth Abbe and the entire staff of The Connecticut Historical Society, to Jeffrey Kaimowitz and Margaret Sax of Watkinson Library at Trinity College, to Judith Schiff, Pat Bodak and the staff of Mss. and Archives, Yale University Library, and to the staffs of the Connecticut State Library Archives, The Mansfield Historical Society, Beinecke Rare Book and Manuscript Library at Yale University, Resources of American Music History at the University of Illinois, and to Anne Schnirel, Mary Beale Kenyon, Richard Crawford, Cynthia Blake, Warren Steel, Rachel Hammerton, Chris Bickford, Alma Browne, Vanessa Wilson, Sue Soterakos, Douglas Wilson, and Robert Keller.

Professor Nicholas Temperley of the University of Illinois and Kate Van Winkle Keller read the final manuscript and were generous with valuable advice and constructive suggestions. Judy Dawson efficiently typed the final copy. Professor James Wilson of the University of Hartford is gratefully recognized for his expert, patient, and liberally-rendered service as "in-house" editor.

RUTH M. WILSON

I

The State of the Art

Music at Mid-Century

To the Reader,

The following Discourse was delivered at a Lecture for the Encouragement of *Regular Singing,* a comely & Commendable Practice; which for want of *Care* in preserving and skilful *Instructors* to revive, has Languished in the Country till it is in a manner *Lost and Dead;* Yea has been so Long Dead, as that with some it *Stinketh;* who judge it a great Crime to use means to *Recover* it again.

BUT however that which is Regular and Virtuous, may thro' the Injury of Time and bad Opinion of unthinking People, seem Tarnished for a season; yet carries such a Lustre with it as is sufficient to Recommend its self to Unprejudiced and Judicious Persons.

From *The Duty of GOD's Professing People, in Glorifying their Heavenly Father; Opened and Applyed, IN A SERMON Preached at a SINGING-LECTURE,* in Hartford, East Society, June the 28th, 1727.[1]

In this sermon the Reverend Timothy Woodbridge (Harvard, 1675), eminent pastor of Hartford's First Ecclesiastical Society, added the weight of the printed word to his efforts to bring order into worship. For that was, in essence, the ultimate goal of clerical exertions toward institution of a new way of singing the psalms "in time of Public Worship." David P. McKay and Richard Crawford have noted that

> it is one of the ironies of American musical history that New England religious leaders advocated the skill of note-reading as a guarantee of musical uniformity. For by the 1760s that skill had become just the opposite: an agent of musical diversity.[2]

There were other factors besides the spread of musical literacy which contributed to a proliferation of musical activity in Connecticut's public and private life. The singing schools in towns and villages, Yale College's artistic leadership, and the increased quantities of books and instruments all had their effect. Equally profound in their impact on Connecticut's cultural life were the social upheavals connected with the Great Awakening, the concomitant divergence of denominationalism, the development of economic diversity, the growth in population, the settlement of outlying areas of the colony, and a release of energy that seemed to transform the quality of Connecticut life.[3] The strict regulation of society by civil and ecclesiastical authority which had prevailed in the seventeenth century no longer dominated politics, government, or religion. Early in the century, however, religious discipline was still viewed by the Standing Order as a means of social control. Nowhere, in the eyes of the clergy, was the lack of order and discipline any more glaring than in the performance of the psalmody in Sabbath meetings. When one considered the "Irregularitys that do attend this part of worship,"[4] the state of congregational singing in the 1720s demanded reform.

Timothy Woodbridge, by his own designation "a Faithful and Aged servant of JESUS CHRIST," did not hesitate to be counted among those "whose Province it is to Guide & Lead in the things that Pertain to the House of God. . . ." He acknowledged as well that "in General the hands of the *Learned, & more Knowing* part of the country are with them in this work; who need no other Testimony but their own Observation of the great Difference in Particular Congregations (no Two Scarce agreeing) as to the mode of Singing, to satisfy them that 'twill quickly run it self into *a meer Jargon* unless it be Reduced to the Standard."[5] Thomas Clap, Yale president (1741-1766), offered another argument for uniformity in his essay addressed to the central question, "Whither yᵉ Regular way, is so much better than yᵉ usual way, as yᵗ it is worth while to be at yᵉ Pains of a general Reformation?"

> Those That sing by Rule sing all Alike [he wrote], & can joyn in any Congregation yᵗ sing so, whereas in many Congregations where they sing yᵉ usual way they cannot; for having of late neglected to sing by the Psalm-book (Tis granted by all) that each Congregation hath taken up a Perticular way of their own which they are pleased to call The Old Way but I am sure that it is impossible that our Fathers when they first came into this Land should have as many old ways as there are Congregations in New England.[6]

Clap's personal experience apparently convinced him that uniformity was the more practical and attainable alternative.

> Singing by Rule is so easy That all persons whither Natural Singer or no may learn it; where as a great many serious Persons can never learn to sing by Rote
> That all persons may learn to sing by Rule is evident from Reason, for all yᵗ are not idiots may learn to Read or to Cypher or the like and from Experience for I have known several Persons who have been counted yᵉ most destitute of all konoledge in Musick & could never so much as pretend to follow in the Usual Way have made considerable Progress in Singing by Rule; But many serious persons do constantly affirm & we have Reason to believe them That yy cannot learn to sing by Rote & So are deprived of much of the benefit of that Part

of worship it has been before granted that it is the duty of all persons to sing but all persons cannot sing by Rote and thefore they must Sing by Rule for God does not obliege men to Impossibilities.[7]

Running through every essay, sermon, and lecture promoting Regular Singing was the reminder that it represented an authoritative and venerable tradition. As Clap put it:

Singing by Rule is the true Old Way because the Tunes & ye Rules are to be found in ye Psalm-book [the Bay Psalm Book] & other books above 100 years old; whereas there is no mention of ye usual way in any old book in ye World; but it came Gradually into the Churches, occasioned by persons Setting up their own Fancies & neglecting the Psalm book.[8]

Here is the crux of the matter in the clash between old and new. The bitterness of controversy over the adoption of singing "the Tunes as they are prick't down in our Psalm-book" was, for most Connecticut congregations, a fierce struggle between two traditional practices. One of these was grounded in written music, performed according to the rules, and giving the notes of the melody their proper pitch and length. The other evolved without benefit of books. The tempo of singing slowed down gradually over time, each singer decorated long notes of the tune with additions of his own choosing, and the performance became highly individualistic in its musical elements.[9]

Usual-way singers took refuge in the belief that their forefathers sang as *they* did, and that that was the true ancient way. Reformers countered by going farther back into recorded history for the beginnings of a written music tradition. Nathaniel Chauncey, for example, stated that

As for the Original of Musick, *That* was before ever there was a Papist, or a Church of *Rome* in the World. It was in great Request and Flourished much in *David's* time; *David* himself was excellently Skilled in Musick, and so were many others in his time. And it is plain it was in use in *Moses's* time; and probably known and used before the Flood.[10]

"Popery" or "Papist" were favorite epithets dredged up since the Reformation to fuel attacks on elaborate or learned church music, especially the cathedral music of the Church of England. They served as well against Regular Singing. Another fashionable charge was that "this practice leads to the Church of England and will bring in Organs quickly."[11] Later on, one Connecticut man who was opposed to Regular Singing concluded his protest by "going over" to the enemy. The story was related to Ezra Stiles in Providence in 1772 by the future Divinity Professor of Yale College, the Reverend Dr. Samuel Wales:

When Mr. Wales was here he told me, that soon upon his Settling [at Milford, Connecticut, December, 1770] a wealthy Member of his Church took offence at New singing—by himself, called Ten Councils—got no Satisfaction—and has now gone over to Church of England.[12]

It is only fair to point out here that by that time the Church of England in Connecticut had grown in numbers of adherents as well as in reputation.

During the Puritan Commonwealth in England, 1644-1660, a death blow to "Popish" custom was a matter for rejoicing. One Puritan sympathizer noted (1646) that there was

A most rare and strange alteration in the face of things in the cathedral church at Westminster. Namely that whereas there has wont to be heard nothing almost but roaring boys, tooting and squeaking organ pipes and the cathedral catches of Morley, and I know not what trash; now the popish altar is quite taken away, the bellowing organs are demolished and pulled down, and the treble, or rather trouble and bass singers, chanters or enchanters driven out, and instead thereof, there is now set up a most blessed orthodox [Puritan] preaching ministry. . . .[13]

The writer's aversion to part-singing reflects the Calvinistic doctrine that only unaccompanied, unison congregational singing was proper in worship. This view prevailed in New England, too. Thomas Clap implied that two-part singing had been tried as well.

Obj: But some may say they don't love to hear the sound of the Base, I answer A thing that a Person is unaccostomed to may seem strange at first, but all that understand the base or have been used to hear it think it is a great Ornament to the Musick—

2 There are many Persons who have not Voice shrill enough to sing the Treble without taking a great deal of Pains and so must either Sing the Base or (many Times) nothing at all

3 The Treble & Base is sung by Rule by our Brethren the Presbiterians in England & Scotland as appears by their Books, & the Testimony of those that come from thence,

4 It was formerly sang here because it is prick't out in the Old Editions of our Psalm-Books; & *some now alive Remember the singing of it.*[14]

Who these persons were who remembered singing bass and treble is not clear. If they were Congregationalists, the "Old Editions" would have been the Bay Psalm Book, after 1698; the ninth edition was the first with a supplement of tunes, notated in tenor and bass. "Our Psalm-Books" usually referred to the Bay Psalm Book. Tate and Brady's *New Version* was in circulation, too, and a supplement with the 1700 edition printed the tunes with treble and bass parts.

Thomas Clap's essay and, for that matter, the whole controversy over two traditional musical practices raise many questions which call for some background information. The religious musical tradition which Connecticut's early settlers brought with them to their new homes had its roots in sixteenth-century continental Europe—France, Germany, and Switzerland—and in England. The singing of metrical psalms was a feature of English Protestant worship from the time of the Reformation. The practice developed among English exiles in Frankfurt, Geneva, Emden, and Strasburg during the reign of Roman Catholic Mary I (1553-1558) when the Reformation in England was temporarily reversed. After Elizabeth I came to power in 1558, the exiles returned to England, bringing their enthusiasm for psalm-singing with them. Unaccompanied metrical psalm-singing had been tried out at the Strangers Church in London, established in 1550 to accommodate Protestant exiles from the Continent. Similar experiments may have been tried in English churches. The Queen's Injunctions of 1559 permitted the singing of a song or hymn at the beginning or end of Common Prayer, morning or evening. Metrical psalm-singing at these prescribed times became very popular, both in parish churches and in the cathedrals, although it was not a part of the liturgy.[15]

The predominant influence on musical practice came from the reformed churches of Calvin and Zwingli. In Germany, Luther approved of the singing of newly-written hymns to the old chorales and some secular tunes, but Calvin taught that only divinely inspired scripture was suitable for singing in worship. The distinction between hymns and psalms was not arbitrary, although it may seem so in this day and age. One of the major decisions made by many eighteenth-century Connecticut congregations was whether to allow "in time of publick worship" the use of a new version of the psalms. The admission of hymns was even more controversial, and hymn-singing did not replace psalm-singing until the nineteenth century in some places in England and America.[16]

Calvin's aesthetic principles about music in church have, consciously or unconsciously, guided generations of Protestants. They provide a framework for early New England practice. Calvin believed that

> it must always be looked to that the song be not light and frivolous but have weight and majesty, as Saint Augustine says, and there is likewise a great difference between the music one makes to entertain men at table and in their homes, and the psalms which are sung in the Church in the presence of God and His angels.
>
> . . .
>
> Now among the other things proper to recreate man and give him pleasure, music is either the first or one of the principal, and we must think that it is a gift of God deputed to that purpose.
>
> . . .

13

And in fact we find by experience that it has a secret and almost incredible power to move our hearts in one way or another.

. . .

Now in speaking of music I understand two parts, namely, the letter, or subject and matter, and the song, or melody. It is true that, as St. Paul says, every evil word corrupts good manners, but when it has the melody with it, it pierces the heart much more strongly and enters within; . . . Now what is there to do? It is to have songs not merely honest but also holy, which will be like spurs to incite us to pray to God and praise Him. . . .

. . .

Wherefore, although we look far and wide and search on every hand, we shall not find better songs nor songs better suited to that end than the Psalms of David which the Holy Spirit made and uttered through him.

. . .

Now the peculiar gift of man is to sing knowing what he is saying. After the intelligence must follow the heart and the affection. . . .[17]

Calvin recommended unison, unaccompanied singing of the Psalms of David in metrical translations because he did not consider prose chanting of psalms, as performed by cathedral choirs, suitable for or manageable by the people. The difference between prose psalms and metrical psalms is a distinction of kind as well as of execution. Metrical psalms were "a utilitarian device, based on devotion to the letter of God's word, aiming merely to cast it into measured and rhyming lines which plain people could sing to simple melodies, as they sang their ballads."[18]

Chanting of prose psalms belongs to the liturgical tradition of the Church of England. Besides the psalms, cathedral music included chanting of other portions of the liturgy, settings of canticles, and anthems. While metrical psalm-singing was allowed and heard in both cathedral and parish churches after the Injunctions of 1559, it was the only music in most parish and country churches. There, metrical psalms were sung by the congregation, unaccompanied, led only by a parish clerk.[19] It is this practice which was duplicated on this side of the Atlantic in the first New England settlements.

According to Thomas Clap's description, about 1725,

Our fathers wn they first came over into this Land in Plymouth Colony sung Ainsworth's Psalmbook Boston Colony they sung ye Church of England Psalmbook Till ye year when President Dunstan [Dunster] (who was afterwards Minister at ye north End of Scituate) did with the assistance of some other ministers Compose our Psalmbook, & the Tunes were for the most part taken out of Ainsworth & ye Old England Psalmbook, & put into ours with Rules & directions how to sing them, & they remain there to this day to be ye Rule & Standard for Singing, which I never heard denied by anyone.[20]

14

The immediate source of the tunes with their basses in the Bay Psalm Book (9th edition, 1698), or New England Psalm Book, as it came to be known, was John Playford's *Introduction to the Skill of Music* (London, 1679 edition).[21] This influential book "remained the standard English text on the rudiments of music for more than a century,"[22] and it served as a model for American psalmodists throughout the eighteenth century. One of Connecticut's earliest-known singing masters, George Beale, owned a copy.

Of the other two books Clap cites, Ainsworth and "ye Church of England Psalmbook," only the second was known to have been used in Connecticut. This was Sternhold and Hopkins, *The Whole Book of Psalms . . .* (London, 1562), which appeared in over 500 musical and non-musical editions from the sixteenth to nineteenth centuries. The "Old Version," as it was called, was never officially adopted by the Church of England, but it carried the weight of authority according to a traditional belief that the word "allowed," in the Injunctions of 1559, meant sanctioned for exclusive use.[23] It was still in use in New Haven First Society in 1762,[24] when many Connecticut congregations had changed over to either Watts' *Psalms of David Imitated* (London, 1719) or Tate and Brady's *New Version of the Psalms of David* (London, 1696). Ezra Stiles noted that the *New Version* was used in 1761 by Congregational Societies at Killingworth (Dr. Eliot), Norwich (Mr. Lord), and New London (Mr. Byles).[25] Most Church of England parishes used the *New Version* as well. It, with Sternhold and Hopkins, was popularly believed to have been published under imprimatur of the Church of England.

Teachers, ministers, and some, but by no means all, members of a New England congregation owned psalm books. Illiteracy also restricted participation in the musical portion of public worship. To circumvent this problem, the Westminister Assembly in England (1644) directed ministers, or someone appointed for the purpose, to read the psalm, line by line, before it was sung. John Cotton reiterated these instructions for New Englanders in his treatise, *Singing of Psalmes a Gospel-Ordinance* (London, 1647):

> The last scruple remaining in the manner of singing, Concerneth the order of singing after the Reading of the Psalme. For it is doubted by some and concluded by others, that reading of the Psalmes is not to be allowed in order to singing. We for our parts easily grant, that where all have books and can reade, or else can say the Psalme by heart, it were needlesse there to read each line of the Psalme before hand in order to singing. But if it be granted, which is already proved, that the Psalmes to be ordinarily sung in Publique, are Scripture-Psalmes, and those to be sung by the body of the Congregation. Then to this end it will be a necessary helpe, that the words of the Psalme

be openly read before hand, line after line, or two lines together, that so they who want either books or skill to reade, may know what is to be sung, and joyne with the rest in the dutie of singing;[26]

Uppermost in official concern was the prescription that everyone should understand the words of scripture through singing. The procedure of having a line or two of text read by someone before it was sung by the congregation is called "lining" or "lining-out."

Church records sometimes present a confusing picture of elected officials and their responsibilities in formal worship. In addition, accounts were kept in many different individual styles, in hands belonging to persons of varying literary ability. Titles varied as well. In Church of England parishes, a distinction was sometimes made between society clerk, or record-keeper, and parish clerk, or psalm-leader. The title of deacon in Congregational societies was often held by two persons, and only one functioned as precentor (one who played or sang before, according to Webster.) The title of chorister was assigned to a precentor as well as to choir members. The terms "set" or "tune" the psalm consistently referred to the precentor's task. In Ashford, for example, "our brother John Perry" was selected "to set the psalm with respect to public singing."[27] New London's meeting voted, "that for the benefit of setting the psalm Mr. Fosdick is seated in the third seat at the end."[28] Farmington chose Elijah Cowles "to Tune the Psalm on Sabath Days and other meetings of Publick worship and that he shall sit in the fifth Pew."[29]

Later on, groups of singers who had learned note-reading objected to being scattered around the congregation. Requests for special choir seats often became a heated issue between Regular-way and Usual-way singers. The almost sacrosanct nature of seat allotments in the meeting house made the assignment of special seats for singers understandably upsetting to conservatives. As Oscar Zeichner has pointed out, "although the souls of the elect might be equal in the eyes of God, their bodies in Connecticut were consistently ranked and rewarded on the basis of such selective criteria as family background, wealth, religious affiliation, and apparent godliness."[30]

Descriptions of legendary characters who served as deacons, clerks, or choristers suggest that many brought to their positions a measure of imagination and energy. One can only conjecture how much recognition was afforded to a musical leader because of his special musical talents or how much was due to other trappings of elected office.[31] The deacon's authority was normally highly respected, as a case in the First Ecclesiastical Society in Woodstock shows:

March 8   1749/50

To hear and consider ye Complaint of Jonathan Payson, a member of this chh against Deacon John May, a member of this chh; In whh Complaint sd May is charged with having publickly asserted, yt. sd Payson had opposed him in Tuning or setting ye Psalm, and afterwards before several persons denied ye words by him spoken, whh in ye opinion of ye Complainer is inconsistent with ye truth, and therefore moves that Deacon May be required to make publick satisfaction to all he has offended, by Charging & Denying as aforesd . . . [The lengthy argument proceeds with admonishments to both parties.]

5 Tho we do not determine, that by ye Gospel Rule, Brother Payson was obliged to deal privately with Deacon May for what he had publickly delivered yet his denying, as in ye Complaint supposeing it was a Crime, yet it was not at first a publick Crime, and therefore we judge yt according to Mathw 18. 15—18 Brother Payson ought to have taken more private measures with ye Deacon before he had brought that part of his Complaint; and that his omission is not to be Justified nor Imitated.

6 It appears Brother Payson has at sundery times; when Deacon May tuned ye Psalm, discovered manifest signs of uneasiness whh is all, yt Deacon May says he meant by Intimating his having opposed him in Tuneing ye psalm.

Teste. Abel Stiles Pastor[32]

The Society, sitting as a court, upheld Deacon May.

Psalm-setter Henry Brace of Hartford West Society apparently fell victim to the idiosyncracies of an aging minister rather than to congregational dissatisfaction with his musical leadership. The Society's records provide no firm reason why the minister, Benjamin Colton, deposed him, but the congregation, in this instance, went along. The matter was handled in the following manner:

Janry 24, 1753

After some discuss Relating to the Case of Mr. Henry Brace about Singing

Voted that we are unesey at Mr. Colton's putting him down from Singing or Seting the Psalm for ye Society

Voted to Chuse a Commity to treat with Mr. Colton on Sd afair

Voted Thom Hosmer Esq.r & Capt. Danll Webster & Dea con Wm Merrill & Isaac Goodwin & Ebenezer Sedgewick to be a commity to treat with Mr. Colton on Sd affair in if the matters of uneseynes Between the Society & Mr. Colton can be acomodated

[Meeting adjourned]

Febry 6, 1753

Voted that wee are yet unesy in the Case of Henry Brace being put down from Seting the Psalm

Voted Cap^n Hosmer Left Jacob Kellogg & Cap^n Dan^{ll} Webster Be a
   Com^y to Go to Mr. Colton to treat with him on S^d Affair
Voted that if Mr Colton will send it up in writing to Be Read to this
   meeting that his Resentments were Raised too high & continued
   on too long—or if he will come personaly to the Meeting & say so
   or will say it in the Meeting house they will accept it
The Commity Returned with a paper from Mr. Colton
Voted to accept of what Mr. Colton has said as Sattisfaction.[33]

Henry Brace's dismissal did not permanently end his service to West
Society, since he reappeared as psalm-setter in the records of the next
decade. The case demonstrates, nevertheless, the way business was
usually conducted between a Society and its minister, who "was at once
the leader, and the servant of the congregation. While he was not
subject to any discipline and control from above, he confronted his
'superiors' every Sunday when he faced the congregation."[34]

The degree of musical specialization of clerks, deacons, or choristers and the extent of their influence cannot be known with certainty.
Each church was a separate political entity, and, from the earliest days
of settlement, "in matter of ecclesiastical polity, creed, and discipline,
the Connecticut churches adhered in all respects to the New England
way of the churches. . . ."[35] There, as in town meeting, parochial
decision-making prevailed. In fact, town and church government were
the same for much of the early colonial period, as symbolized by
Enfield's town minutes (1704/5) which record that "nathaniel horton
is chosen to set ye salm tunes on ye publick, & Isack pese when he is
absent."[36] Gradually, the functions of town and church governments
diverged, but decisions affecting worship practice were still thrashed
out in the New England way.

A case in point is the discussion and vote in a meeting of Windsor's
First Society in 1736 on whether Deacon Marshall's "Old Way" of
singing would continue in public worship, or whether Mr. Beal's new
"Singing by Rule" would be adopted. A show of hands proved to be
inconclusive, "there being many voters," so the Moderator "ordered
all of the voters to go out of the seats and stand in the alleys, and then
that those that were for Deacon Marshall's [way] should go into the
men's seats, and those that were for Mr. Beal's way should go into
the women's seats. . . ." Objections to this method were put down
by the Moderator, and the hand count was taken again, this time by
the Moderator and the clerk, Henry Allyn. The Moderator got a total
of 63 or 64, and Allyn counted 42. They counted again and agreed on
43. "Then the Moderator was about to count the number of votes for
Mr. Beal's way of Singing called 'by Rule,' but it was offered whether
it would not be better to order the voters to pass out of the meeting-
house door and there be counted." Again objections were raised, but

the Moderator ordered it to be done, and Deacon Marshall's supporters complied and were counted at 44 or 45. Mr. Beal's supporters were asked to

> draw out of their seats and pass out of the door and be counted; they replied they were ready to show their minds in any proper way where they were, if they might be directed thereto, but would not go out of the door to do the same, and desired that they might be led to a vote where they were, and they were ready to show their minds which the Moderator refused to do and thereupon declared that it was voted that Deacon Marshall's way of singing called the 'Old Way,' should be sung in Public for the future, and ordered me to record the same as the vote of the said Society, which I refused to do under the circumstances thereof, and have recorded the facts and proceedings.[37]

The matter was finally settled several years later when Mr. Beal's was was voted in and Deacon John Wilson was elected to "tune the Psalm" and Deacon John Cook to "read the Psalm."[38] Hartford's West Society chose Jacob Bidwell to "set the psalm" in 1761, and the next year, voted that "Noah Webster [Senior] Read the psalm for this Society" and that "he Set with Mr. Bidwell the Corister."[39] These examples highlight the problem of clarifying the roles of both leader and congregation, and later on, the choir. How lining-out was actually done in churches where it took place is still open to question, although survivals of the tradition in southern American churches are believed to be similar.[40] That lining-out was widely practised is verified by church records and by accounts such as a letter in the *New England Courant,* complaining that

> The same person who sets the Tune, and guides the Congregation in Singing, commonly reads the Psalm, which is a task so few are capable of performing well, that in Singing two or three staves the Congregation falls from a cheerful Pitch to downright Grumbling; and then some to relieve themselves mount an Eighth above the rest, others perhaps a Fourth or Fifth, by which means the Singing appears to be rather a confused Noise, made up of Reading, Squeaking, and Grumbling, than a decent and orderly part of God's Worship. . . .[41]

Theoretically, the singing was in unison, but in practice a kind of heterophony developed, with some voices going along at the interval of a fourth or fifth, possibly a sixth above, the tune. This process, which Nicholas Temperley has called "popular harmonization," came about with the introduction of popular singing in worship following the Reformation.[42]

The Old Way of Singing gradually became slower, and people embellished the tune in their own way by filling in intervals with notes and turns or trills. Nathaniel Chauncey called it a "loose, irregular way" that had become so popular that "we are now grown in love with it." Singers in the Old Way "readily Grant that they use many Quavers and Semiquavers. . . ."[43] A psalm-tune collected in the nineteenth century in Scotland is a good illustration.[44]

FRENCH TUNE

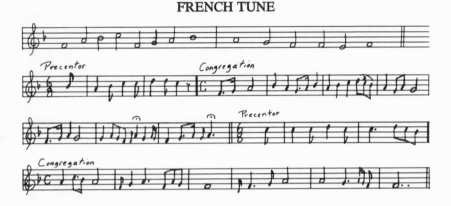

The custom of embellishing a plain tune, handed down as part of an inherited repertory, created a highly ornamental, individualistic idiom. Allen Britton has formulated the hypothesis that "this unschooled manner of singing was closely allied with the folk song of the period, of which little is now known."[45] This popular song was likely to have been the ballad, which originally denoted a dance song.[46] Ballads circulated in oral tradition as well as in print. As broadsides, ballads were printed on one side of an unfolded sheet. Usually only the text appeared, sometimes with a designation for a favorite tune, and sometimes without reference to specific music. "The broadside ballad . . . was a kind of musical journalism, the forerunner of the popular prose newspapers, and continuation of the folk tradition of minstrelsy."[47] Story-telling and song-singing were popular amusements in colonial Connecticut. One such entertainer ran afoul of the law, stole a horse in Goshen, New York, and headed for Boston via Hartford. Jonas Dubois advertised in the *Connecticut Courant* of May 27, 1765, for the return of his property and the thief, Henry Gore, "an Irishman, about 6 feet high, and slim, pitted with the small-pox, hallow ey'd, wears his own hair, had on a blue coat, and a jacket figur'd in imitation of seal-skin; he is something talkative, a great story-teller, card-player and a song-singer. . . ."[48]

The folk ballad tradition may well have furnished the songs Gore sang. A clue to their melodic features may be found in the writings of Regular-way reformers who linked the Usual way with non-worship song-singing. Nathaniel Chauncey's reference to embellished tunes concludes with the remark that "all these Musical Characters belong wholly to Airy and Vain Songs; Neither do we own or allow any of them in the Songs of the Lord."[49] Thomas Symmes wrote that "most of the *Psalm-Tunes* as Sung in the *Usual way,* are much more like *Song-Tunes,* than as Sung by Rule; . . . more *Supernumerary* Notes & Turnings of the voice. . . ."[50] If this ornamental psalm-singing style were close to songs sung for recreation, enjoyment, entertainment of friends and family, and social conviviality, the reluctance to give it up in worship is all the more understandable.

According to Alan Lomax, some traits of song performance show powerful relationships to features of social structure. In an environment strictly regulated by governmental authortiy, the Usual way provided people with an opportunity for expression within prescribed limits of general acceptance. Singing in worship was a Christian responsibility, both individual and collective, and as such carried the weight not only of religious tradition, but also of congregational necessity. The moral obligation is clear in Thomas Clap's words:

> 1 That Singing is a Part of Y^e Pub^l: Worship & That it is ye Duty as well privilige of al Persons to joyn & assist in it, & therefore it is a Sin (at least for those y^t think it is a Duty) to be silent in y^t Part of Worship unles there be some Just Impediment.[51]

Song style, states Lomax,

> portrays some level of human adaptation, some social style. Each performance is symbolic reenactment of crucial behavior patterns upon which the continuity of a culture hangs, and is thus endowed with the emotional authority of the necessary and the familiar. Moreover, many levels of this symbolic behavior are brought into congruency with some main theme, so that a style comes to epitomize some singular and notable aspect of a culture, by which its members identify themselves and with which they endow many of their activities and their feelings. This is why an expressive style may become the focal point for cultural crystallization and renewal.[52]

By seeking to reform the expressive style, Regular-way enthusiasts attacked, in the belief of Usual-way singers, their cherished prerogative. "The Tempers of some have been so high, as that it has driven them on to turn their Backs on the Mode of Singing at the time of *Publick Meeting,* as if it were some Idol Worship . . . ," commented Woodbridge.[53]

The Regular way, or Singing by Rule, eventually won out everywhere. Some Connecticut churches adopted the new way in the 1720s, some in the 1770s. In Wallingford, the Society voted in 1731 to "agree to Sing in ye public assembly in ye Sabbath half ye time in ye new and half in ye old way for six Sabbaths; and after that wholly in ye new way."[54] Lebanon Crank (now Columbia) followed their neighbor's example, and voted (1737) "to sing in the public worship according to the rule by which they sing in the old Society in Lebanon."[55] The Town of Glastonbury directed the First Society in February 1733 to sing half the time by rote and the other half by rule. This apparently did not work out well, for a Society meeting in July of that year voted that Regular Singing be deferred until the following December. Meanwhile, a program of singing meetings was held at specified intervals and places so inhabitants could "learn the said way of singing."[56]

In Hartford, despite the leadership provided by the Reverend Timothy Woodbridge and the Hartford Association,[57] Regular Singing was not officially adopted in the First Society until after Woodbridge's death. The Society voted in June of 1733 that they were "willing and Content that Such of them as Encline to Learn to Sing by Rule should apply themselves in the best manner they can to gain a Knowledge thereof."[58] They decided to try Regular Singing after three months and until the next December, when they voted again and agreed "that singing by Rule be admitted and practiced in the Congregation of this Society in their publick Worshipping of God."[59] The systematic way in which several Hartford-area towns handled the reform issue suggests the possibility that the General Association was setting down guidelines. The Reverend Nathaniel Chauncey's sermon, *Regular Singing Defended* . . . , delivered before a General Association meeting on May 12, 1727, was published with the approbation of the Association, signed by the moderator, T. Woodbridge. Singing lectures for the purpose of teaching were held, and the sermons preached on those occasions were printed and distributed.

In one area town, the adoption of Singing by Rule was anything but smooth. Farmington First Society voted in April of 1724 to delay its admission, and two months later, they decided to take a year's time to investigate the new method. In addition, they voted "that if any person or persons shall presume to sing contrary to the lead of the Quoirister appointed by the church to the disturbance of the assembly, and the jarring of their melody, he or they shall be looked upon and dealt with as offenders."[60] Captain Joseph Hawley responded to a fine for breach of Sabbath by petitioning the General Assembly that

> Deacon Hart the chorister one Sabbath day, in setting the Psalm, attempted to sing Bella tune, and your memorialist being used to the old way as aforesaid did not know *bellum* tune from *pax* tune, and supposed the Deacon had aimed at Cambridge short tune and set it wrong, whereupon your petitioner raised his voice in the said short tune and the people followed him, except the said Smith and Stanley and the few who sang aloud in Bella tune, and so there was an unhappy discord in the singing as there has often been since the new singers set up. . . .[61]

The similarity in the opening phrase of the two tunes shows how confusion could arise.[62]

BELLA   CAMBRIDGE SHORT

The people were not to blame for good intentions, said Josiah Dwight, pastor at Woodstock, in a sermon entitled *An Essay to Silence the Outcry that has been made in some Places against Regular Singing* (1725):

> And I see not but some Congregations, and Sundry in many more, are to be blamed for their ignorance and heedlesness about the Tunes, that may be can't distinguish one Tune from another when sung, and slide out of one Tune into another, and do not mind it, or Sing the Lines of several Tunes for one: when a little care & study inded would have saved the Disorder.[63]

This Old way of singing, with its improvised "popular harmonization," Dwight proposed to "correct" by having the deacon "name the tune together with the Psalm and all the Skilful of the Congregation be sure to fall in with the first Note & Syllable. [This proposal was not] without Experiment; for some of us have been some time in proof hereof, and see its Expediency." Lining-out would be dispensed with, of course, by this method.

"Since the new singers set up" in Farmington, however, experiments in regular singing ran into the proverbial brick wall.

> Att A Society Meeting in y[e] first sociaty in ffarmington, march y[e] 17[d]: 1726/7: this meeting taking late Consideration [of the] unhappy controversies that hath been amongst us Respecting Singing of Psalms in our public assemblies upon y[e] sabaths, and for as much as the Church in this place, hath several times in theyer meetings manifested theyer dislike of singing Psalms according to y[e] meathod not long since endevered to be introduced amongst us being y[e] same way of singing of Psalms which is Recommended by y[e] Reverend Minesters of Boston with other minesters to y[e] Number in all of twenty or theyr abouts. Therefore that y[e] s[d] Controvercys may be ended and peace gained to this sociaty, this meeting by theyer major vote Do declaer theyer full sattisfaction with y[e] former way of singing of Psalms in this sociaty and Do earnestly Desire to Continue therein, and Do with y[e] Church manifest theyer dislike of singing according to y[e] meathod intended to be Introduced as afors[d]:[64]

"Ye Reverend Minesters in Boston" were the Harvard-trained leaders of the reform movement, which began there about 1720. Thomas

Symmes' influential pamphlet, *The Reasonableness of, Regular Singing, or, Singing by Note,* appeared in 1720. Thomas Walter's *The Grounds and Rules of Musick* Boston, (1721) and John Tufts' *A Very Plain and Easy Introduction to the Singing of Psalm Tunes* (3rd edition, 1723, extant) provided Farmington's musical innovators with tunes and directions for singing. It appears, nonetheless, that they were definitely in the minority.

Timothy Edwards' firm leadership in his East Windsor congregation led to a vote for regular singing in May of 1727, "according to the rule of singing now brought in, and taught among us by Mr. Beall."[65] According to his descendant, Mary Beale Kenyon of Wethersfield, George Beale came to Connecticut about 1725 with his sons, Matthew and William. Beale had acquired his musical training in the "old country." While a guest at Edwards' house when teaching in the East Windsor Society, Beale made regular visits to Hartford, Springfield, Willington, and "to ye West Side of ye River &c."[66] Matthew followed his father's occupation and was active in New Preston, Woodbury, Windsor, Hartford, and other towns before he moved to Long Island prior to the Revolution.[67] When George Beale's will and inventory were recorded in 1761, his son was in possession of his horse, saddle and bridle, and most of his music books, which are listed in the following portion of the inventory.[68]

Singing schools usually met for a number of evenings each week, for a period of from two weeks to several months. In Glastonbury, instruction was arranged for once a month at the meeting house and once a month at three separate dwellings in different parts of the town. Some schools were believed to have met in taverns, where there was enough room for teacher and students. The singing master taught the rudiments: the Gamut or scale, rules for finding mi, musical characters, moods of time, lessons for "tuning ye voice," and pieces for performance, mostly psalms at first. Students copied their lessons into their own blank commonplace books. "Much of the instruction was based on manuscript materials,"[69] the printed psalmbooks, and the instruction books of Tufts and Walter.

At Yale College, a classical musical education was taught, befitting the young gentlemen who would be Connecticut's civic and religious leaders. Textbooks and curriculum were the same as at Harvard College, where the Boston leaders in Regular Singing received their musical training.[70] Rector Elisha Williams (Harvard, 1711), a regular-singing advocate, was in college at the same time as John Tufts (Class of 1708) and Thomas Walter (Class of 1713).[71] Thomas Clap, Rector at Yale after Williams, was also Harvard-trained (Class of 1722). Under Rector Timothy Cutler and up to about 1730, music at Yale was part of the mathematics curriculum. Music theses were listed under *Theses Mathematicae* in the commencement broadsides for 1723 (3), 1727 (3), and 1729 (4). In addition, three appeared under *Theses Physicae* for 1720; one, for example, was titled *"Diffusio Soni est Sphaerica,"* (Diffusion of sound is spherical). Other examples are:

1727　*Musica est Theoretica et Practica,*
　　　Theoretica est sonorum, temporis et quantitatis respectu relationum, Scien/tia/
　　　Practica de voces modulandi ratione versatur.
　　　Music is theoretical and practical.
　　　The theoretical is the knowledge of sounds, time, and quantities in respect to their relationships. The practical is concerned with the means of modulating voices.
1729　*Musica est Ars, varias Sonorum modificationes docens.*[72]
　　　Music is the Art which teaches various modifications of sounds.

Music theses appear mostly under *Theses Physicae* after 1735, indicating a change in curriculum and textbook to Charles Morton's *Compendium Physicae.* Morton's musical material included acoustics, physiology of the ear, theory of concord and discord, the Gamut or Scale of Music, and aesthetics.[73] A total of 18 theses were listed in the 1735, 1736, 1743-45, and 1753-55 broadsides. Two more are under *Theses Mathematicae* for 1746 and 1749. A thesis from 1735, entitled *"Harmonia et discordia sonorum e proportionibus pulsuum aeris oriuntur,"* demonstrates the physics orientation. This thesis, "Harmony (or Concord) and discord of sounds arise from the proportions of beats of bronze (or of vibrations in the air)," probably refers to the Pythagorean hammers.[74] According to Apel, "Pythagoras is said to have discovered the basic laws of music by listening to the sound of four smith's hammers, which produced agreeable consonances."[75] From their weight, 12, 9, 8, and 6 pounds respectively, Pythagoras derived the octave, fifth, fourth, and whole tone ratios.

Tutor Ezra Stiles' notebooks for 1749 contain several music lessons: one on the Latin solmization syllables, one on musical aesthetics, and one entitled "Musick." It begins with the statement, "Every Vibration of a Chord excites a Wave in the Air—. . ." and goes on to discuss the tension of chords and their vibration ratios, adding the interesting comment that "the Distance of the Waves of the Sound, with which we pitch our unison Tunes in Vocal Musick; is about 4 feet."[76] In a different kind of note on vocal music, Stiles copied a verse into his student notebook for 1745:

> Sternhold & Hopkins They had Qualms,
> When They translated David's Psalms,
> To make our hearts right glad:
> But if 't had been St. David's Fate
> To hear you sing & them translate
> By Jove 't would 've made him mad[77]

The Bay Psalm Book, it may be recalled, was intended to improve Sternhold and Hopkins' translation of the psalms from the original Hebrew. So was Tate and Brady's *New Version.* The music printed with the standard psalmbooks and in Tufts' and Walter's many editions supplied the literature for a growing tradition of choral music in Connecticut during this period. Two additional tune supplements, by Turner and Johnston, were printed in New England in the 1750s.

The psalms were also the musical mainstay on a variety of private and public occasions. Domestic psalm singing was a very old custom dating back a century or more. At home, four-part music with instrumental accompaniment may have been performed. Family worship usually included psalms in a program of prayer and catechism. Besides Sabbath and Lecture-day services, there were religious ceremonies connected with public holidays like election, thanksgiving, and fast days, and probably training days, too.[78] Vocal music had its prescribed place in all of these proceedings.

Psalm singing was as much a part of life at Yale College as everywhere else in the colony. The first commencement in Yale's new college building in 1718 featured the usual prayer, orations, and disputations, and concluded, as was customary, with vocal music. On this august occasion were sung four verses of Psalm 65, perhaps, as Dexter suggested, in Sternhold and Hopkins' translation, "Thy praise alone, O Lord, doth reign, In Sion thine own hill."[79] John Sargeant gave his Valedictory Oration at the Yale commencement in 1729, addressing his classmates with a "picture to hang on memory's wall": "How often have the walls in echos reverberated the tuneful notes of praise we with united voice and heart have sung to our great creator and Redeemer."[80] The practice of vocal music was undoubtedly looked upon as a healthy activity for young men, just as the singing school was sanctioned as a proper place for young people of a town to meet in "mixt" company. For Yale students, there was the added obligation of preparation for leadership, and part of that training, especially for ministers, was music. Rector Elisha Williams, who came to Yale in 1726, had a reputation as "a great friend to Regular Singing."[81] The place of music as the servant of religion was succinctly summarized by Cotton Mather in his directions to ministerial candidates:

> For MUSIC, I now not what well to say. Do as you please, if you *Fancy* it, I don't *Forbid* it. Only do not for the sake of it Alienate your Time too much, from those that are more Important Matters. It may be so that you may serve your GOD the better for the Refreshment of One that can play well on an Instrument. However, to accomplish yourself at *Regular Singing,* is a thing that will be of *Daily Use* to you. For I would not have a day pass you without *Singing,* but so as at the same time to make a *Melody in your Heart* unto the Lord, besides the Part you may bear, In Hymnis suavisonantis Ecclesiae.[82]

The musical repertory did undergo some changes and additions before the 1750s, despite the predominance of unison or harmonized, block-chord psalm settings. John Cleaveland's diary, kept in his freshman year at Yale, mirrors a variety of convivial occasions, each livened with its own brand of music making. For example,

> Jan 21 [1741] . . . After supper they sang of some of Dr. Watts' Hymns.
> 15 This day is Fryday . . . After I came home I and Whilliams sang a Hymn and that there came up five more And we sang a hymn and so the departed . . .
> 23 This night we had a meeting in Hawley's room and we sange first and then prayed twice.
> March 4 . . . This night a coris was attended by some of the scholars & in the Reverend Rector's house—
> 5 . . . This night the soformores and freshmen had a coris: O the dessolation of Sion—
> 12 . . . This night the soffermores had a coris in copp's room.[83]

Hymn-singing in the manner of Cleaveland and his friends was a common feature of private gatherings for discussion and prayer, especially in the revival atmosphere of the 1740s. The custom may be related to earlier religious societies of young men, formed to encourage the practice of psalmody.[84]

The "coris," however, may have performed other kinds of vocal music than the traditional psalms or hymns. Printed music for airs, songs, and choruses was available in English collections like John Playford's *Introduction to the Skill of Music,* D'Urfey's popular *Wit and Mirth, or Pills to Purge Melancholy* (1719-1720), Watts' *Musical Miscellany* (1729-1731), and Bickham's lavish *Musical Entertainer* (1738-1740). Broadsides and songsters, collections of song texts to be fitted to melodies known in the popular repertory, were in circulation as well. The "coris" in the home of Rector Clap could have been for recreational psalm singing, but it could also have introduced more elaborate religious choral music of the kind then being published in England. British psalmodists, following Henry Playford's model in *The Divine Companion* (London, 1701), were printing anthems which became more complex in texture as time went on. Texts set were the psalms or Scripture passages in prose. Fuging-tunes, with imitative sections, were favorites of later compilers and composers. Rector Clap's *Catalog of Books at Yale Library* (1743) listed two important music books under "Treatises on Various Subjects." One was Playford's *The Whole Book of Psalms,* the source of Tufts' and Walter's three-part psalm settings in *An Introduction to the Art of Singing Psalm-Tunes* and *Grounds and Rules of Musick Explained.*

The other music book, John Arnold's *The Compleat Psalmodist* (London, 1741), was extremely influential, especially on composer/compilers of the second half of the century. *The Compleat Psalmodist* was arranged in four books: Book I, An Introduction to the Grounds of Music; Book II, A Set of Services, commonly called Chanting-Tunes, together with Four and Twenty excellent anthems, composed of Solo's, Fuges, and Chorus's; Book III, The whole book of Psalm-Tunes; Book IV, A Set of Divine Hymns; the whole composed for from one to five voices. As the titles indicate, the musical style was not restricted to traditional psalm settings.

Of wider consequence was the devotional poetry of the English Dissenting minister, the Reverend Isaac Watts. Clap's *Catalog* lists *Horae Lyricae* (1705), *Psalms of David* (1719), and *Hymns* (1707), all part of Watts' donation to Yale College library in 1730.[85] These volumes, along with Watts' *Divine Songs for Children,* "formed the very heart of American psalmody and hymnody for the second half of the century."[86] Watts' versification was the product of a conscious desire to personalize the Christian experience. His paraphrases of the psalms related them to the history of his own time in language that was easily understood. In Louis Benson's words, the process was one of "making David speak like a Christian and making him a contemporary of Watts."[87] The second process was "surely Watts' own conception."[88] This helps to explain why those who considered the psalms sacrosanct might look upon any paraphrase of Scripture as sacrilege. Even so, and especially after the Great Awakening, Watts' *Psalms* became the definitive version for succeeding generations. Many Connecticut churches adopted Watts' *Psalms* officially soon after mid-century. Hartford West Society was probably one of the first, for on April 18, 1748, they "voted to *Continue* the Use of Doc[t] Watts his version of the psalms for our publick worship."[89]

Watts' *Hymns and Spiritual Songs* supplied freely-composed texts for a kind of congregational song which was capable of expressing any Christian sentiment or emotion. They were particularly popular among congregations touched by the revivals of the Great Awakening. Their metrical structure meant that they could be sung to an appropriate tune already in the common repertory. Although not officially accepted into worship at first, they were sung at many other meetings, such as those John Cleaveland described at Yale. Hymn-singing took on the function in larger meetings of creating a receptive attitude for the preacher's words. Singing could signal the first step toward conversion. Jacob Eliot, an "Old Light," reported in his diary for March 28, 1742, that "after public worship P.M. a company of young men set to singing to draw the people together to prepare for Exhorting, &c. I stilled 'em & persuaded the people to go home."[90]

Hymns worked a powerful influence on the preachers of the Great Awakening, as their diaries, journals, and letters witness. A typical day on the preaching circuit was described by Eleazer Wheelock, minister, missionary, and founder of Moor's Indian School: October 24, 1741, "Rose early, prayed and sang. Discoursed with some wounded; afterwards exhorted a company, who came in. Sung a hymn, prayed, and rode with a great company of Voluntown people and others to Providence . . . ."[91] Separatist preacher Elisha Paine, from Canterbury, wrote in a letter to his family, "after service we sang a hymn. I felt the spirit of the Lord come upon me. I rose up and exhorted and persuaded them to come to Christ; and immediately there was a screeching and groaning all over the multitude . . . ."[92]

These outpourings of mass "enthusiasm" were anathema to the Standing Order. Itinerant preachers, in the eyes of the established church, were the harbingers of public confusion and purveyors of disorder in the body politic. Their musical predilections came under censure as well. The *Declaration* against James Davenport by Massachusetts Bay ministers on June 28, 1742, contained the following:

29

We judge also, that the Rev. Mr. Davenport has not acted prudently, but to the disservice of religion, by going with his friends singing through the streets and highways, to and from the houses of worship on Lord's days and other days. . . .[93]

Davenport's outdoors music violated several codes which governed musical usage. Singing while moving about in the town was a long way from grave and solemn psalm-singing in the meetinghouse, especially on the Sabbath! The musical character of the hymns, if that is what was being sung, must have had some bearing on the censure.

Each form of musical expression had its place, dictated by the nature of the event. The ordination of a minister is an example of a personal, family, Society, and community affair that enclosed seemingly disparate musical practices. The ordination ceremony itself was conducted with appropriate formal solemnity. Pastor Daniel Wadsworth of Hartford described one in which he took part on October 4, 1738:

> This day y[e] Rev[d]. M[r]. Andrew Batholomew was ordained paster of y[e] Church and people at y[e] Town of Harwinton according to y[e] direction of y[e] ordination Councel. I began with prayer, y[e] Rev[d]. M[r]. Whitman of Farmington preached from Jer. 3. 15. and made y[e] prayer previous to y[e] charge, and gave y[e] charge, y[e] Rev[d]. M[r]. Marsh made y[e] next prayer, y[e] Rev[d]. M[r]. Whitman of Hartford gave y[e] right Hand of fellowship and y[e] part of y[e] 118. psalm was sung and y[e] Rev[d]. M[r]. Bartholomew pronounced the blessing.[94]

A feast, and sometimes an ordination ball, followed the ceremony. An invitation, in his own handwriting, to Timothy Edwards' ordination ball (1698) was in the possession of a descendant of the recipient in the last century.[95] Frances Caulkins, nineteenth-century historian of Norwich and New London, commented, "An ordination ball, strange as it may sound, was allowed in some places as a finale to the festivities on the occasion of settling a minister: but there is no proof that this enormity was ever perpetrated in Norwich."[96] This Victorian judgment does not alter the fact that dancing was an acceptable form of amusement in the right place and time. As Oscar G. Sonneck has pointed out, "the Puritans, the Pilgrims, the Irish, the Dutch, the Germans, the Swedes, the Cavaliers of Maryland and Virginia and the Hugenots of the South may have been zealots, adventurers, beggars, spendthrifts, fugitives from justice, convicts, but barbarians they certainly were not."[97] Ministers in Edwards' time were social and civic leaders, and their clerical positions did not exclude them from the leisure activities of vocal and instrumental music-making and dancing.

Similarly, a New Haven General Court case against John Clearke and his friends was not because of the activity, but primarily for violation of curfew. Stephen Bradley admitted "to singing & soe set them to daunce,"[98] and Clearke confessed

. . . that he had beene two or three times at John Brownes house in
yᵉ evenings with some others . . . where there was dauncing & once
playing at cards: did further Confesse that his maine ground of
goeing away was, that he might goe where he might have more liberty,
for one from Connecticut told him if he lived there he might live
merrily & sing & daunce &c. [At this date, 1662, Connecticut and
New Haven were still under separate governments.][99]

These dances were undoubtedly country dances, popular everywhere
in the mother country and the colonies, and collected and published by
John Playford in *The English Dancing Master* (London, 1650/1).[100]
They could be performed with or without instrumental accompaniment,
or to singing, or even to the ubiquitous and ancient jew's harp. The
jew's-harp or trump, an article of barter in the seventeenth century,
has a frame which is held in the player's mouth and vibrates while an
elastic strip is plucked by the player's fingers. It is thus a combination
of instrument and "mouth music," and since it requires no great technical skill and was available in quantity in Connecticut, it no doubt was
in wide use.[101]

The tunes for country dances came from the same fund of melodic
material drawn upon for ballad operas, topical songs, military marches,
and ballads. A typical example, engraved with its music about 1740
in London, was

The Rakes of Mallow for yᵉ German Flute

Beauxing belling dancing drinking	Spending faster then it Comes;
Breaking Windows daming sinking	Beating bawds Whores and Duns;
Ever Raking never thinking	Bacchus true begotting Sons;
Lives the Rakes of MALLOW.	Lives the Rakes of MALLOW.[102]

The melody was printed with the figures of a country dance in *A Choice
Collection of 200 Country Dances, Vol. 3* (London: Jno. Johnson,
1744) and was the indicated tune for the fifth air of the ballad opera,
The Conspirators (London, 1749).[103] Major Christopher French, a
British war prisoner in Hartford in 1775-76, wrote twelve verses en-
titled "French's Maggot" to the same tune;

1. Come my Boys, let's merry be
   Let's laugh & sing, be full of Glee
   Although we've lost our Liberty
   Confin'd in Goal [sic.] at Hartford.
2. We'll skip about, dance merry Jiggs
   In spite of all pretended Whiggs
   As lively be as any Griggs
   Although in Goal [sic.] at Hartford.[104]

In 1777, military fifer Giles Gibbs of Ellington copied the tune down by ear in his commonplace book, calling it "Rakes of Marlow Quick Time."[105] The tune is still current.

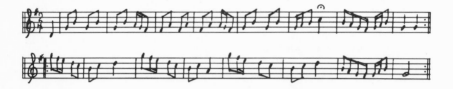

The violin was the favorite instrument for the dance. Professional musician and teacher, George Beale, owned a "viel enn," and may have taught the latest dances, as did Edward Enstone, a European musician who emigrated to Boston in 1714 as organist for King's Chapel and subsequently opened a school as Master of Music and Dancing.[106] In Litchfield, "the first use of the violin . . . for a dance was in the year 1748. The whole expense . . . did not exceed one dollar; out of which the fiddler was paid."[107] This fiddler was probably a servant from a Litchfield household, and a large number of later newspaper advertisements for runaway musicians, carrying an instrument with them, gives evidence of their value as well as their existence. Jeremiah Platt of Hartford offered "FIVE HUNDRED DOLLARS REWARD . . . [for] a likely Negro Man, named Bill, about 25 years of age, 5 feet 6 or 7 inches high, plays well on the flute and fife; . . . is supposed he will attempt to get to New York, or within the enemy's lines . . . ."[108] Abda Duce, servant of Captain Thomas Richards, owned his violin and left it to his wife, Lidia, at his death in 1708/9.[109] The Reverend Jonathan Todd, pastor of Guilford East Society and one of Connecticut's largest slave-owners, was reported to have "so expert a fiddler that on many occasions [he] invited the young people of the village to his house 'to hear Tom play on his fiddle.' "[110]

Violinists played concerted music as well as dance tunes, and private music-making could have been the reason Captain John Livingston of Norwich owned a violin.[111] Colonel John Benjamin, Jr., prominent Stratford town official and organist of Christ Church for many years, most definitely played chamber music at home. His father's inventory includes a dulcimer, and he owned several instruments, among them a violin and a spinnet.[112] Yale Tutor Simeon Baldwin, on an excursion to attend a friend's ordination in Stratford, noted in his journal for August, 1784,

—we dined at Esq. Brooks, & closed the day with a very good Ball— the next day dined at Mr Stebbins Quarters—took Tea at Dr Johnsons [William Samuel] & spent the Evening most agreeably at Mr Benjamins —entertained with a variety of music.—[113]

The use of musical instruments by pragmatic Connecticut colonists extended not only to leisure activities, but also to communications, the regulation of the daily routine, and military training and defense. The drum, a percussion instrument made of materials readily at hand, was selected for the widest variety of tasks, and its player, normally the town drummer, became crucial to the orderly progression of daily events. His conditions of service were legislated by town meeting according to each town's needs. New London, for example, hired Peter Blatchford in 1651/2 "to beat the drum all saboth dayes, training dayes and town publique meetings for the sume of 3 lb., to be paid him in a town rate."[114] The duties of the drummer and the town constable were frequently combined. There were often two drummers, one for military and town meetings, and one for church meetings, in which case, care of the meeting house was commonly part of the latter job. Windsor, at town meeting on May 16, 1678, hired Baggot Egleston for "the cleansing of the meeting [house] for this year coming for 50s, and the beating of the drum to meetings for 28s," having previously paid Walter Gaylord for "beating the drum and new cord" £1.1s.[115] Accounts for 1668/9 include payment for "Drum and drum head. 3s."[116]

On October 3, 1650, the New Haven General Court decreed that "Nathaniel Kimberly is appointed drumer for ye towne and is to have [£] 5[1] a yeare wages, he maintayning his owne drume."[117] That accounts for the higher wage. By March 21, 1652, a new drummer, Ephraim How, was chosen, since Kimberly, "who did supply the place," was gone. How was directed to "attend the publique occasions of the Towne for druming . . . and keepe his drume in repair at his own charge, it being so put into his hand, and is so to leave it when he shall leave the worke; . . . and for his service being faithfully performed, he is to have seven pound a yeare, wch yeare is to begine this day: . . ."[118] Public service meant announcing meetings, accompanying the watch to and from the watch-house, calling hours such as 9 o'clock curfew, raising "alarum" in times of danger, marking cadence for military training exercises, and performing such special functions as closing auction sales "at the beat of the drum to the highest bidder,"[119] and playing early in the morning during the season for burning the ox pasture to warn men "to goe to secure their fence from the fire."[120]

An invoice made by the townsmen on February 1, 1657, showed one drum in use, and two spare new heads and two old rimms, "secured from damage, as followeth: Ther is one drum in use wth Tho. Kimberley, and 2 spare heads. Ther is two drum rimms and an old head in the prison."[121] In 1660/1 a new drum was ordered, to be "provided at ye Town charge, the Treasurer to pay for it, ye Military officers to procure it."[122] "It was left to the Military officers to provide a drummer."[123] This was logical, since the drummer was responsible for signalling the training maneuvers of the militia. In the Code of Laws, (1644),

> . . . it is ordered that all the Soulgers within this Jurissdiction shall bee trained at least six times yearely, in the months of March, Aprill, May, September, October or November . . . theire meeting together shall be at eight of the clock in the morninge.[124]

The "Clarke" was ordered to keep track of arms, ammunition, drums, and colors, and to take roll and levy fines for absence. From a total fine of two shillings six pence per man, the clerk was authorized to take six pence for himself "and the remainder for the maintenance of Drums, Cullers &c."[125] A snare drum made in the seventeenth century is still in existence in possession of the Connecticut Historical Society. The Farmington drum, as it is known, was handed down in the William Porter family and given to the Society in 1843. An ancestor, Samuel Porter, was town drummer in the first decade of the eighteenth century. The drum measures 24½ inches across and is 19½ inches deep. Only the shell, elaborately studded with brass tacks and bearing the letters L D, is extant. The Farmington drum is similar in size to "a drum of the Elizabethan period still in existence which measures 22½ by 22¾ inches."[126] Drums were not of standard size, "since the foot was not a standard of measure at the time, but literally the size of the human foot."[127]

The drum provided the cadence for the march of foot soldiers. There were two basic cadences in the British Army, the common step and the quick step. Militia training, patterned after British manuals and techniques, would normally have used the common step for marching exercises.[128] The drummer conveyed "signals and commands by means of recognizable patterns or pre-arranged drum rudiments."[129] By the seventeenth century, the names of the calls "seem to have become standardized . . . these names and functions have continued practically unchanged to the present.[130]

> Call—to assemble, to hear proclamations
> Troop—to arms
> March—march to beat of drum
> Preparative—ready to execute first command
> Charge—press forward
> Retreat—orderly retiring
> Chamade or Parley—with enemy
> Reveille—beat in morning, double signal for guards to cease challenging and others to rise and prepare for work
> Tatoo—played at evening, soldiers to retire, taverns to close.[131]

With troops of horse, a trumpeter called the signals. On March 11, 1657/8, the first troop of horse in Connecticut colony was authorized by the General Court in Hartford. Captain John Mason of Windsor

THE FARMINGTON DRUM

Courtesy of The Connecticut Historical Society

was in command. By 1741, after reorganization of the militia, a troop of horse was authorized for each of thirteen regiments. Ceremonial occasions such as state funerals would, of course, call for the full complement of military musicians. Joshua Hempstead of New London described the funeral of Governor Gurdon Saltonstall in his diary entry for September 22, 1724:

> . . .
>
> ye Troop & Capt Latimers & Capt Christophers (being ye first & Second) Companys in N. London Attended in Arms. ye 2 Lt a brest Led & Captns brought up Coll Whitting att ye Head to order Horse & foot. Marcht all in 4 files. Drums, Coulers Trumpets Hal[berts] & Helts of officers Swords being Covered with Black from ye Govrs Gate to ye Tomb. . . .[132]

A tolling bell would have been heard in any town able to afford its purchase. Bells were imported before foundries were established in the colony in the 1730s (Abel Parmele in Guilford) and 1740s (John Whitear in Fairfield, 1744). New London had installed a large brass bell, at a cost of £25, in the 1690s, purchased from a merchant in the City of York, England. The sexton's wages for ringing it were 40 shillings, added to his annual salary of £3.[133] Stratford may have had the first bell in the colony, for the 1660 town records state: "That Goodman Pickett shall take the place which Goodman Peake, for age hath layd downe in ringing the bell: . . . They do alow unto him [£] 2 10 s. to be paid yarely."[134] New Haven's prolonged town meeting discussions in the 1680s over the purchase and proper use of a bell point up the careful consideration given to the change from one musical instrument to another as a means of ordering community life.

It is reasonable to suggest that, besides economics, the acoustical properties of instruments, as well as their symbolic or customary meaning, had some bearing on their use. Windsor, in the 1650s, put both military instruments to the purpose of calling meetings on the Sabbath and on lecture days: "Capt. Cook shall cause that seasonable warning shall be given to come to meeting . . ., by Drum or trumpet, on the top of the meeting house. . . ."[135]

Whether called by trumpet, drum, or bell, Connecticut's early settlers came to meeting to hear their minister preach, and to add their own voices in singing of the psalms, their "gospel Ordinance." The strength of the psalm-singing tradition supported the community in its work and in its recreation. Whether vocal or instrumental, music was interwoven in the fabric of daily life in important and constructive ways. As Connecticut arrived at the mid-eighteenth century, this was no less a fact. Diversity replaced homogeneity, both in society and in the cultural manifestations of that society. Musical life and musical traditions changed and adapted themselves to new environments in myriad ways. Musical culture however, continued to be an integral part, as it had been from the very beginning, of Connecticut society in all its diverse elements.

II

Twenty Years Before Lexington

"New pieces of Music"

A THANKSGIVING HYMN,
for New Engand.

New-England, raise thy grateful Voice,
   Thy sweetest Notes prepare,
In Songs to Heaven's Almighty King,
   The God of Peace and War.

'Twas He our pious Fathers led,
   To seek a Savage Land;
And Heav'n born Liberty that fled
   A Tyrant's fierce Command.
. . .

He gave our populous Towns to rise,
   With thousand Fold Increase;
Our Desarts into Gardens turn'd;
   Our Navies fill'd the Seas.

Louis, beheld the rising State,
   Indignant, and design 'd
With Chains of Slavery and Rome,
   Our Happy Coasts to Bind.

But God appear'd for our Defence,
   Our Foes were turn'd to flight,
Amherst and Wolfe, 'twas He inspir'd
   With all their dreadful Might.
. . .

In songs of Praise to Britain's God,
   Let all her Subjects join,
And may our Lives, and Voices prove
   A Harmony divine.

From the *Connecticut Gazette*, New Haven, November 1, 1760.

A SHORT-LIVED euphoria pervaded the colonies at the end of the French and Indian War. The years which intervened before Lexington were characterized by rapid political and economic change and by far-reaching social ferment. Population growth alone created intense pressures in several directions, causing the settlement of outlying areas of Connecticut, as well as the migration to burgeoning urban communities such as Hartford, New London, and New Haven. Such centers "now became small cities and took on many of the attributes of urban life."[1] Other complex factors contributed to the secularization of life and to sectarian multiformity in the wake of the Great Awakening. An increasing diversity of occupation and an influential merchant class altered the social and economic balance.

Much of the eighteenth century until the Peace of Paris in 1763 was dominated by war-time conditions. Society functioned, therefore, within a persistent framework of shifting relationships, both personal and collective, public and private. Sources of information multiplied with commercial and community proliferation. Carl Bridenbaugh has observed that

> Improved communications with the mother country, partly normal and partly in response to war needs, speeded the transfer of European ideas and culture to the colonies. This accelerating transit of civilization is evident in the whole range of urban activities and was primarily caused by the coming of the British Army and by the steady stream of immigrants arriving on these shores.[2]

The rural hinterland was similarly affected, as people and ideas moved back and forth across the territory now known as the State of Connecticut. It has been likened to a cask of liquor, drawn on at each end by New York and Boston, with little left in between but "lees and settlings."[3] This clouded image hardly does justice to Connecticut's busy society, even though Boston and New York did serve as centers of fashion and sources of goods for Connecticut people. Lathrop and Smith, Hartford booksellers, encouraged customers to buy "at home" with a note to their advertisement in the *Connecticut Gazette* (New Haven), "N.B. Said Books will be sold as cheap as They can be purchased in Boston, or New York."[4] Customers could mail order as well.

Those who could not travel easily could read reports in Connecticut newspapers about cultural events elsewhere in New England, in other colonies, and in the mother country. For example, Hartford's *Connecticut Courant* for December 10, 1764, printed a notice from New York of the charity sermon to be preached the next Sunday at Trinity Church and at St. George's Chapel, "a proper Hymn to be sung at Trinity Church, and an Anthem at the Chapel; to be join'd in the Chorus by the Charity Scholars."[5] In the May 26, 1766, issue, Boston's celebration of the repeal of the Stamp Act was reported: "The morning was ushered in with Musick, Ringing of Bells, and the Discharge of Cannon . . . ."[6] New Haven's *Connecticut Gazette* published, in November 1761, the complete order of procession for the coronation of King George III.

New England's early history may have left the impression that Boston was the only major cultural and commercial center before the Revolution, but "as the colonial era ended, Manhattan had whittled down Boston's traffic with this province, especially in the Connecticut and Thames valleys."[7] On a visit to Middletown in 1771, John Adams observed that "The People here all trade to N. York, and have very little Connection with Boston."[8] Cultural influence emanated from both cities, nonetheless, and there was a brisk traffic in ideas and literature, and occasionally an exchange of personnel. The *New York Gazette,* January 14, 1760, advertised:

> This is to give notice that the Subscription Concert will be opened on Thursday next, the 15th instant, at Mr. Willet's Assembly Room, in the Broad Way. N. B. Those gentlemen that intend to subscribe to the said concert, are desired to send their names to Messrs. Dienval and Hulett who will wait on them with tickets, for the season.[9]

Mr. William C. Hulett, actor and dancing and music master, came to America in 1752 as violin player in Hallam's American Company and taught in New York in 1759.[10] He published an advertisement in the New Haven *Connecticut Gazette* the summer following the subscription concert:

> This is to give Notice, that W. C. Hulett, Dancing-Master, from New-York, has opened a Dancing-School in Hartford, where the Minuet and Country-Dances are taught, in the most genteel and shortest method, and on very reasonable Terms. 'Tis hoped those Gentlemen and Ladies that intend doing him the Honour of instructing them, will apply as soon as possible, he being obliged to return to New-York at a limited time.[11]

It was quite customary to encourage business by stating that one could only offer instruction for a limited time, but Mr. Hulett may well have returned to New York for the 1760-61 season. He is not mentioned in any concert notice for that year, so it is also entirely possible that he tried his luck in Connecticut for longer than one summer. He may also have operated a school in Connecticut for the summer season on a regular basis.

Musical merchandise, books and instruments, were readily available from New York and Boston. Mein's London Book Store in Boston solicited mail order business from Connecticut residents through a two-page advertisement in the New London *Connecticut Gazette* (1767). It offered:

. . .

Free-Mason's Pocket Companion . . . to which is added, a large
Collection of the best Masons' Songs, . . .
Tate & Brady's Psalms
Watt's Psalms and Hymns

. . .

Psalmody William's Psalmody	Tansur's Royal Melody compleat
—Anthems	Arnold's Church Music
Green's Psalmody	—Harmony
Arnold's Complete Psalmodist	Bayley's Introduction to Music . . .

Songbooks	The Masque	Frank Hammond's Songs, or every
	The Warblers Delight	Buck and Choice Spirits Com-
	The Bucks do—a	panion
	Coll of very	
	humerous Songs	

. . . A Collection of Songs, very elegantly printed on fine writing
paper, and entirely calculated for the Votaries of Comus.

Tutors for the Violin and German Flute

. . . All the Magazines & Reviews printed in Great Britain . . .
all the Best Plays and Operas in the English language . . . At
the very same Price they are sold at in London.

. . . Mein imports regularly, all the new Publications in every Art
and Science; . . .

. . . Gentlemen, Traders &c. who send Orders, may depend on
being served with the utmost Fidelity and Dispatch, and as
cheap as if present.

Those who buy to sell again are allowed a considerable discount.[12]

The last was directed to the ubiquitous itinerant pedlar as well as to the local storekeeper. Timothy Green's advertisement for books and pamphlets in the *New London Summary* (1762) closed with the statement, "Country Traders, &c. who take a Quantity, will have a good Allowance made them."[13]

Books found their way into households throughout the colony, either through inheritance or purchase. Estate inventories listed, besides the prized family Bible or psalmbook, libraries ranging from a few volumes to many hundreds. John Adams, always the careful observer, looked into his chamber closet one morning while staying with friends at Stafford Springs and "found a pretty Collection of Books, the Preceptor, Douglass's History, Paradise lost, the musical Miscellany in two Volumes . . . ."[14] At Shaylors' in Middletown, Adams again found the "musical Miscellany" among a few books in a little bedroom.[15] This song collection was likely *The Musical Miscellany, being a collection of choice songs, set to the violin & flute* (London: John Watts).[16]

The newspaper advertisements placed by Connecticut printers and bookdealers in the 1750s included most frequently a psalmody-related selection limited to Walters' *Grounds and Rules of Musick*, Tate and Brady's *New Version*, and Isaac Watts's *Psalms and Hymns* and *Divine Songs for Children*. From the mid-1760s on, they reflect a wider local market for the extensive selection of music books that Mein's Boston store offered through mail order. In a list headed by the usual Bibles, psalters, primers, and psalmbooks, the New London Printing Office advertised in the summer of 1768 the latest British church music collections: *e.g.*, "Tansur's Melody [*Royal Melody Compleat*, 1755]–Knap's Psalmody [William Knapp, *New Church Melody*, 1753]–Arnold's Church Music [*Church Music Reformed*, 1765]– Leicester Harmony [John Arnold, *The Leicestershire Harmony*, 1759]– Bayley's Church Music [*The American Harmony*, 1767]."[17] The latter was a combination of two English books, Tansur's *Royal Melody* and Aaron Williams's *The Universal Psalmodist* (1763), published by Daniel Bayley in Newburyport, Massachusetts.

The repertory of plain psalm tunes and settings of psalms, hymns, and prose texts (anthems) in Bayley's compilation served as a model for many New England composers. Josiah Flagg's two mid-60s collections of British psalmody were also influential in New England.[18] Significantly, young Connecticut composer and teacher Amos Bull proposed to publish selections from British psalmodists and some new pieces in 1766, before Bayley's similar tunebook came out. By the end of 1769, Lathrop and Smith in Hartford were featuring music books, not just including them at the end of a long list of other kinds of literature.

SINGING-BOOKS
TO BE SOLD BY
LATHROP & SMITH,
In Hartford, viz.

Tansurs Royal Melody Compleat at
5/4 single, or 5/ by the dozen—Williams's universal Psalmodist at 7s—a new edition of Arnolds compleat Psalmodist, with
large additions printed in 1769, at 7s—And
a new edition of Knibbs Psalm Singers help,
with large additions at 5s all on a good paper,
and well bound.
    They have also a large assortment of
other books, which they will sell cheap for
Cash, Pork or Grain in hand.[19]

Song books were also available at local printers. The New London Printing Office sold, besides church music collections, the *Vocal Companion* and a *Choice Collection of Songs*. These were likely songsters, containing texts without notated music. Newspaper columns and single-sheet broadsides were the major printed media, however, for the dissemination of the perennially-popular, as well as the newly-composed, topical song-text. These were written to commemorate, illustrate, or comment upon a current event. Verses were often intended to perform a political function, either as parody or propaganda. Much of this poetry was designed to be sung to a well-known tune from the common repertory. A tune title was sometimes printed with the text, or a refrain or chorus might suggest the writer's intention. The wedding of text and tune was usually calculated to capitalize on the associations, in terms of meaning and structure, which surround a traditional song or ballad. An inexhaustible source of textual material could be found in the swiftly moving political and military events of the moment. When dramatic words in company with the right popular tune created a memorable musical and pictorial image, a successful "New Song" took its place on the colonial "hit parade."

Victory on the battlefield could always be counted on to stimulate new verse production. The highlights of the French and Indian war were no exception. The political hymn (page 43) in the traditional ballad meter (common meter, 8.6.8.6.) provided a neat summary. An earlier "Cheer for Soldiers and Sailors," offered in the pages of the *New London Summary,* was "humbly addressed to his Royal Highness Prince Edward, the Rising Protector of the British Navy: and [was] to be sung or said on board all His Majesty's ships, transports, &c. going to the coast of France." Each verse of six lines began with a catch phrase interspersed with key color words.

> Verse 1—Come, come my lads, away to France
>   Let's shew the French an English dance,
>   . . .
> Verse 2—Courage, my boys; up to the nose,
>   (The French are our invet'rate foes)
>
> Verse 3—Not life, but liberty we prize;
>   And so does ev'ry man that's wise.
>   . . .
> Verse 4—Or should we die a sacrifice
>   T'our country's laws and liberties.[20]

The routine progression of the monarchy, as well as the vagaries of political leadership, were commemorated in verse. When George III ascended the British throne in 1760, the major battles of the French and Indian War were over, and he fell natural heir to a war hero's mantle. The *New London Summary* printed an enthusiastic adulation in the form of a hymn "compos'd to be Sung upon His Coronation-Day." The language of the first two lines, "The Lord now tune our Hearts to Sing, And bless His Name for George our King," became more martial in successive verses with references to the "Guardian-Hero" with the "Sword of Justice in his Hand." The hymn returns to an affirmation of divine right in its last verse.

> Verse 6—Angels, to you our prince is known,
> Loud did you shout Him on the Throne,
> Aid Albion's Sons, with one accord,
> To join the Shout, and praise the Lord.[21]

This hymn can be sung to any Long Meter (8.8.8.8.) tune, such as the familiar "Old Hundred."

The last verse of John Dickinson's "Liberty Song," written in 1768, still paid lip service to the British king with the lines, "This bumper I crown for our sovereign's health, and this for Britannia's glory and wealth . . . ." The next lines continued, however, with "That wealth and that glory immortal be, If she is but just, and we are but free."[22] The political climate had clearly undergone a series of modulations by 1768. John Dickinson, the author of *Letters from a Farmer in Pennsylvania,* wrote his "Song for American Freedom" as propaganda.[23] He appealed for unified opposition to British taxation in the words, "No more such sweet labors Americans know if Britons shall reap what Americans sow." Dickinson selected the tune, "Hearts of Oak," which in turn became the second most popular tune for topical songs of the American Revolution.[24] "Hearts of Oak" was a song composed by English cathedral musician William Boyce, for actor David Garrick in his pantomime, *Harlequin's Invasion* (1759).

HEARTS OF OAK

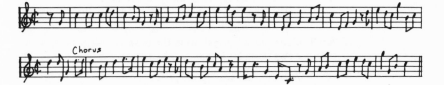

For a political song, the tune is not as immediately singable as one with more step-wise motion and without a modulation to the dominant at the end of the verse, but the sturdy scalar march of its first two phrases, the dramatic octave jumps which close the verse and the chorus, and the outline of the chordal structure in the chorus make it distinctive and memorable. "Hearts of Oak" was written as a topical song, and the opening of both it and the "Liberty Song" are very similar in feeling despite their differences in wording.

"Hearts of Oak"
Come, cheer up, my lad, 'tis to glory we steer,
To add something more to this wonderful year,

. . .

"Liberty Song"
Come join hand in hand brave Americans all,
And rouse your bold hearts at fair Liberty's call;

. . .

The words of the chorus provide a unifying thread in many of the texts written to "Hearts of Oak." Dickinson changed the original "Steady, boys, steady" to "Steady, friends, steady." The complete refrain says:

In freedom we're born and in freedom we'll live;
Our purses are ready, Steady, friends, steady,
Not as slave but as freemen our money we'll give.[26]

The "Liberty Song" provides a good example of the speed with which new song texts travelled. It appeared in Pennsylvania in a broadside and in the *Pennsylvania Chronicle,* July 4-11, 1768; the *Boston Gazette,* July 18; the *Virginia Gazette,* July 21; the New London *Connecticut Gazette,* July 22; and on September 3 was printed in the *London Chronicle* in England.[27] The "Liberty Song" was a rare case in which the music was printed with the words.[28]

An allegorical song on the governors of Connecticut is preserved among the Trumbull papers at the Connecticut Historical Society. No extant published copy has been located, but the manuscript dated October 10, 1769, appears to have been copied from a broadside. It is a typical product of the period, except that it shows evidence by its wit and style of being a more polished literary effort than the usual political song. The parody technique of the topical song-text is plain. The original "Vicar of Bray" was supposedly connected to the post-Restoration period in English history, when the state religion changed with the monarch on the throne. The anti-clerical writer of the Connecticut ballad lamented the changing character of succeeding governors of Connecticut colony. He used the rhyme scheme, part of the original chorus, and the same tune to evoke the flavor and sense of the original. The tune is related to the one now known as "Country Gardens."

VICAR OF BRAY

A comparison of the first verse of the original "Vicar of Bray" and the anonymous Connecticut parody demonstrate the technique. John (line 2) is Governor Winthrop, Connecticut's first governor. Line 5 refers to the colonies of New Haven and Connecticut before their union.

Parody

In sixteen hundred sixty-two,
When John, the first, was Pilot
Our ship was rigg'd, well-trimm'd
and new,
And sail'd as clean as a fly-boat,
The Crew, tho' cull'd from different
ships,
Each gloried in his Charter,
And with one voice did celebrate
The Son of the Royal Martyr.
And this is what I will maintain
As long as life shall be, Sir,
That I will ever laud him most,
Who does most good to me, Sir.[30]

Original

In good King Charls's golden Days
When Loyalty no Harm meant
A furious High Church man I was
And So I gai[n]d Preferment
Unto my Flock I daily preach'd
Kings are by God appointed
And Damn's are those who dare resist
or touch the Lords Anointed
And this is Law I will maintain
unto my Dying Day s^r
That Whatso ever King shall Raign
I will be Vicar of Bray Sir.[31]

Composing poetry and collecting new verses written by others were fashionable eighteenth-century pursuits, particularly for those whose social positions allowed time for leisure. The Reverend Mather Byles, II, for example, pastor in New London before his conversion to the Church of England, was a typical amateur poetaster, who traded verses with his sister in the manner of the time.

You seem to take it very much amiss that I did not send you a Copy of that curious Song beginning *Let vulgar Bards* &c and really, Sister, I have but one Apology to make for such a shocking Peice of Neglect: & that is I really thought you would not be able to guess what it was about. I might be mistaken indeed: but if I was, you must excuse me. I will send you another, of a more serious Nature, & I should imagine much better adapted to your Taste. It is sometimes sung at Weddings, after the Ceremony.[32]

A song in commemoration of the Stamp Act riots in Boston, first published August 4th in the *Pennsylvania Journal,* appeared in the New London *Connecticut Gazette* on August 19, 1768. Addressed to the Sons of Liberty, it made use of a numerology associated with the vote in the Massachusetts Assembly, 92-17, against rescinding a circular letter urging united colonial resistance to the Townshend Laws.[33] The caption included a bit of Pitt's speech in Parliament: "The Americans are the Sons, not the Bastards of England; the *Commons* of *America,* represented in their several Assemblies, have ever been in Possession of the Exercise of *this their Constitutional Right,* of GIVING and GRANTING their own Money; they would have been SLAVES if they had not enjoyed it."

The last verse of the song, "Come, jolly Sons of Liberty," to the tune "Come, jolly Bacchus or Glorious first of August," praises the Farmer, John Dickinson, and scourges those on the wrong side of the vote.

> Now, FARMER dear, we'll fill to you,
> May Heav'n its Blessings show'r,
> As on the glorious NINETY-TWO,
> But Seventeen devour—
> Mean abject Wretches!—*Slaves in Grain!*
> How dare ye shew your Faces?
> To latest days *go drag your Chain!*
> Like *other* MULES or ASSES![34]

At a wedding ball held in New London in 1769, so the *Boston Evening Post* reported, "ninety-two gentlemen and ladies attended and danced ninety-two jiggs, forty-five minuets, and seventeen hornpipes. The company retired at forty-five minutes past midnight."[35] The numbers represent strictly political associations rather than stamina on the dance floor. The symbol "forty-five" refers to John Wilkes, who championed American causes in the British Parliament and who was imprisoned for criticizing the King in the forty-fifth issue of his periodical, the *North Briton.*

Yale College's anniversary commencement on September 15, 1769, called forth a lengthy, front-page account and a timely political comment in the *Connecticut Courant.*[36] The Procession to the College chapel began at 10:30, and the morning ceremonies were "concluded by an Anthem, sung by the young Gentlemen of the College." Afternoon exercises closed with "another Anthem." The paper took note that "the whole was conducted with that Decorum which will reflect Honor on the young Gentlemen concerned, and to the utmost Satisfaction of a learned, polite, and brilliant Assembly." The commencement exercises had become a major social and academic event. In the evening a number of gentlemen (whether just 45 or not cannot be ascertained) with hearts glowing with an ardent fire for liberty . . . instead of drinking 45 glasses in honor of Wilkes and Liberty, (as had been customary) drank themselves 45 degrees in extreme DRUNK; which they effected by just 45 minutes after midnight which advancing into the college yard . . . to make their joy as public as possible . . . by BAWLING in concert just 45 times. . . .[37]

The account concluded with the news that a similar late-night concert had taken place at Harvard, and the civil magistrates had intervened. The *Courant* expressed the hope that Yale's celebrating students might not be disciplined, "as it might effectually hinder for the future the town's being serenaded by such sweet concerts of melodious bawling." The students may well have been singing such popular favorites as the "Liberty Song," or perhaps "coris" songs such as "The Tipling Philosopher" and "Advice to the Fair Sex" (Gather Ye Rosebuds while ye may). Benjamin Trumbull (Yale, 1759), pastor at North Haven, wrote words and music to both songs in his music book, the latter in Latin.[38]

From Benjamin Trumbull's Music Book

Private musical entertainments were seldom reported in the newspapers, but glimpses appear in journals and diaries. Boston merchant John Rowe wrote in his diary under date of January 5, 1768, that he spent an evening at Joseph Harrison's in New Haven, where "Mr. Mills of New Haven entertained us most agreeably on his violin: I think he plays the best of any performers I ever heard."[39] Rowe was an experienced concert goer, and his judgment can be accepted as knowledgeable.

John Adams' diary provides references to music-making in Middletown by way of comments about his landlady's son, Nathaniel Shaylor, "now 25 or 26 . . . [who] Is a great Proficient in Musick. Plays upon the Flute, Fife, Harpsicord, Spinnett, &c. Associates with the Young and the Gay, and is a very fine Connecticut young Gentleman."[40] Samuel B. Webb wrote about Middletown's entertainments in a letter to his sisters, who were attending a private school in Boston.

> I arose before Bright Phoebus had made his appearance from his wa'try bed, finished my Business and went directly to Middletown, where I pass'd the evening in Dancing—the pleasure of the lady's Company and Madeira made me again Sam B. Webb. . . .[41]

Merchant William Gregory's return trip from Boston in 1771 encompassed a stop on training day in Killingsworth, where he danced reels and country dances all evening. In his opinion, "the string tormentor executed his part so bad that it proved a very great drawback upon our pleasure."[42] At a more formal occasion in New London in 1766,

> in Consequence, of an Invitation, from Capt. Durell, and the other Officers of the Cygnet Man of War, most of the principal Gentlemen and Others (a few excepted) attended an elegant Ball; in a large Building furnished for that Purpose; where they were very politely entertained, to the universal satisfaction of the Parties present.[43]

Unfortunately, the notice does not mention the performers who supplied the music. It was the kind of occasion, however, that would have called for the presence of a military "band of musick."

Entertainment of a different kind went on at meetings of Yale College's secret literary societies. The Linonian Society, founded in the 1750s, and the Brothers in Unity, in the 1760s, were the seedbeds of theater arts at Yale. Many of the late-century literary school known as "The Hartford Wits" developed their talents as writers and poets in the meetings and exercises of these secret groups. In 1770, John Trumbull's Master of Arts oration, "Essay on the Use and Advantages of the Fine Arts," sounded a keynote for American artistic endeavor. The essay closed with a long poem, "Prospect of the Future glory of America," which was full of such fiery patriotic language as:

> For pleasing Arts, behold her matchless charms,
> The first in letters, as the first in arms,
> See bolder Genius quit the narrow shore,
> And unknown realms of science, dare t' explore;
> Hiding in brightness of superior day
> The fainting gleam of Britain's setting ray.[44]

Secret society meetings gradually moved from evening discussions in students' rooms to plays and dialogues acted out in neighboring communities to performances for selected audiences, followed by dinner and dancing. President Stiles commented:

In both Societies many have had an ardent Desire to act Tragedies & other dramatical Exhibitions at their Anniversaries. They have carried all Things secret in the Anniversaries hitherto. Yet lately invit^g Gent. & Ladies in T^o their Entertainments & dramatic Exhibitions have become of Notoriety no longer to be concealed.[45]

The repertory included dialogues, farces, comedies, and tragedies, some possibly interspersed with music. As Julian Mates, historian of the musical theater in America, observed, most eighteenth-century theater productions placed their stress on music rather than on drama.[46] The programs of public concerts were similarly composites of theater music, especially songs and opera airs, and instrumental music from the chamber repertory.

The concert program reported in the New London *Gazette* in August, 1773, was not a concert at all, but a biting political satire.

MUSICAL INTELLIGENCE
EXTRAORDINARY

In Commemoration of the Alliance between England, France, and Spain, a *Concert* of *Vocal* and *Instrumental Music* will speedily be performed at the *Cockpit Whitehall.*

First Fiddle,	Lord *North*
Cocerto [sic] on the *Hum-strum,*	Lord *Ahsley*
A Bloody March to St. George's Fields, on the *Trumpet,*	Lord *Barrington*
Solo on the *Jews Harp,*	*Jerry Dyson*
Royal Solo on the *Bagpipe,* by the ——————.	

After the first Act, a Song in Praise of the *King*
of *France,* set to Music by the late Duke of
Bedford, will be sung by *Hans Stanley.*
The Song is set to the tune of *"Who has e'er
been at Baldock must needs know the Mill."*

The first stanza is as follows:

Who has e'er been at Versailles must needs know the King;
He's a very swarthy man, wears, a very brilliant ring;
He has snuff boxes in plenty and pictures to bestow,
As the Ministers of George the Third do very well know.

After Act II. The following Air will be sung.

AIR *in* PRAISE *of* HANOVER.

Hanover, thou Land of Pleasure,
Seat of ev'ry earthly treasure,
Thou fost'ring Nurse of British Kings,
To thee we owe our great Georgius,
To thee his *Granny* not so pious,
Nor yet so much in *Leading Strings.*

> After Act III. There will be a Grand Chorus by
> all the Persons in Administration; the words
> as follows:
>
> Then here's to thee, my boy Jack,
> And here's to thee, my boy Gill;
> If we've plunder'd the Nation,
> To secure our salvation,
> We'll plunder her more and more still,
>   Brave Rogues,
> We'll plunder her more and more still.
>
> When the Concert is over, Lord North will
> dance a *Hornpipe,* in order to exercise his limbs,
> in case he should ever be obliged to cut capers
> in the air, for protecting an infamous Alliance
> with a State infamous in the annals of History
> for its perfidy and scandalous breach of faith.[47]

At first glance, cultural life at Yale may have seemed restricted by the charter and laws of 1745 which regulated every aspect of student life, but the rule "that every student shall abstain from Singing, Loud talking and all other Noises in studying time . . ." implied that plenty of singing was going on at other times.[48] Drama likewise became an absorbing leisure pastime, despite college rules to the contrary. As early as 1754, performances took place in taverns in nearby Amity and Milford.[49] At a meeting on April 23, 1762, President Clap and the tutors were obliged to pronounce that

> Ingersall upon pretence of necessary Business got Liberty to go to Milford, & after he had been there some Days, he & a number of Scholars & others went to ye Tavern, & acted a Play, & had a mix'd Dance according to ye Appointment they have made some weeks before. . . .[50]

Fines were levied against the students for the double sin of acting and mixed dancing. Especially frowned upon was the practice of male students putting on "women's Apparel." At the Linonian "anniversary solemnity for the year 1773" at Mr. Thomas Atwater's house in New Haven, the Society's Minutes record that

> . . . Between the third & fourth Acts [of the Lecture on Heads] a musical dialogue was sung between Fenn & Johnson in the characters of Damon & Clora, which met with deserved applause. An Epilogue made expressly on the occasion & delivered by Hale 2d was received with approbation. The musical Dialogue was then again repeated; A Humerous Dissertation on Law was delivered by Mills; & at the request of several Gentlemen who were not present in the former part of the Day the first part of the Lecture on Heads was again exhibited . . . .[51]

The dialogue was probably the duet "Go false Damon, your sighing is in vain" by Englishman Henry Harrington. "Damon and Clora" appeared in London in at least eleven song-sheet editions between 1770 and 1790.[52] It is the first song in Chauncey Langdon's *The Select Songster* (New Haven, 1786). Langdon (Yale, 1786) was a member of the Musical Society at Yale. The *Lecture on Heads,* a satire by George Alexander Stevens, was customarily performed with music between each act.

Spoken dialogues became staple fare at Yale commencements, quarter days, and junior exhibitions after 1770. For example:

> Quarter Day. After Dinner in the Hall, assembled in the Chapel, where were exhibited the following Exercises a number of Gentlemen & Ladies present, viz a Latin Oration; then a Dialogue; an Anthem; a second Dialogue or dramatic representation of the invasion of the Tories & Indians upon Susquehanna led on by Col. Butler, in which Pixley acted the Indian Warrier inimitably; an English Oration; an Anthem Concluded.[53]

According to James Hillhouse, there was even a theater in New Haven in 1774. He wrote to Nathan Hale, "Now we have a School of Drama and a wonderful mechanistic as well as artistic theatre to take the place of a room in a tavern . . . ."[54] Temptation to ascribe a loosening of atmosphere to the end of President Clap's tenure in 1766 is best resisted. Many other factors at work in the general social ferment of the period affected college life.

Public musical performances were not billed as concerts in Connecticut in the pre-war years. Nevertheless, there is some evidence that they were managed in the same way as the plays in pre-war Philadelphia, where civil regulation forbade such "public exhibitions." In the late 1760s, some public performances were advertised as "meetings" and completed their disguise with the preaching of a sermon. The format was the same as the early singing-lectures of the 1720s and 1730s, with the added feature of concerted musical performance. Also, it was customary to complete the term of a singing school with a "singing-lecture," a performance by the newly-trained singers which ideally demonstrated the prowess of the teacher and the skills of the students. These vocal recitals were clearly the antecedents of a still-continuing tradition in private and public music education.

A "meeting" advertised in the *Connecticut Courant* in 1769 featured not only vocal and instrumental music, but also new compositions:

> We hear from Wallingford, that a society of Singing-Masters who have voluntarily associated, with a view to encourage Psalmody in this government, at their last meeting there, agreed to meet at the South Meeting-House, in this Town the first Wednesday of October next, at one o'Clock in the afternoon, when several new peices of Music will be performed, both with voices and Instruments, and a Sermon preached on the Occasion . . .[55]

There was no organ in the Second Society meeting house at that date, so if a keyboard instrument were present, it would have been a spinnet or harpsichord brought in for the occasion. More likely, the "instrumental part" was provided by strings and winds, and possibly by brass instruments as well. There were players in central Connecticut who could have taken part, and a number of singing teachers, who presumably played and taught instrumental music. Although no evidence appears in his personal papers, Andrew Law is reputed to have played and taught the violin and flute as early as 1770.[56]

Law might well have been a participant in the 1769 meetings. He was born in Milford on March 21, 1749, to Jahliel (son of Jonathan Law, Governor of Connecticut, 1742-1751) and Ann Baldwin Law. The family removed to Cheshire, then part of Wallingford, in 1753.[57] Andrew Law joined the Cheshire Congregational Church on July 23, 1769, and in 1771 or 1772, enrolled at Rhode Island College, now Brown University. He was a practising musician and teacher throughout his college years in Providence. A classmate, Solomon Drowne, mentioned in his diary that he went to the college one evening in April, 1772, to hear "Law's scholars sing."[58]

Amos Bull was another likely participant in the 1769 singing-masters meetings. He was born in Enfield on February 9, 1744, and grew up there and in Farmington. He married Lucy Norton of Farmington in 1767 and was in Wallingford in 1769 when their daughter Lucy was born.[59] He probably received his musical training in a singing school. By the time he was 22, he was presumably teaching, since he advertised proposals for an ambitious music book as "A. Bull, Philo Musicae," a professional title adopted by a number of composers and musicians.

The title of the proposed book was a composite of Aaron Williams's *Universal Psalmodist* and William Tansur's *Harmony of Zion*. His announcement in New Haven's *Connecticut Gazette* in the fall of 1766 reads:

PROPOSALS for Printing by Subscription, a Book intitled *The new universal Psalmodist, or Beautiful Harmony of Zion*, containing,

First, A new and correct Introduction to the Rules of Music, rudimental, practical and technical.

Second, A Number of the most celebrated Psalm Tunes, collected from *Arnold, Tansur, Lyon, Williams*, &c. with some entirely new.

Third, A Number of Services, Chants, Hymns, Anthems and Canons, suited to several Occasions, never before printed. The whole are composed in two, three, four, five, six, seven and eight musical Parts, according to the nicest Rules, correctly set in Score for Voice or Organ; and peculiarly adapted to public and private Use. By A. Bull, Philo Musicae.

The Piece is ready and will be put to the Press upon suitable Encouragement. The Price to Subscribers will not exceed *Ten Shillings.* Subscriptions are taken in by Capt. *Daniel Bull* and Mr. *Thomas Green* at Hartford, Mr. *Samuel Green* and the Printer of this Paper in New-Haven, and by Persons in each of the other County Towns.

It is desired that the Subscriptions may be returned to the Author, by the first of *January* next.[60]

The "entirely new" psalm tunes could have been composed by local singing masters. Selections were also to be included from James Lyon's *Urania* (Philadelphia, 1761), the first large American collection with anthems, set-pieces, and new hymn and psalm tunes.

Bull's third category—services, chants, hymns, anthems, and canons—may have reflected, besides his own religious preference and the growth of the Church of England in Connecticut, the direct example of John Arnold's *The Compleat Psalmodist.* Church of England services and chants were included in several English collections which served as models for American composer-compilers, but they were rarely copied in New England collections before 1800. (Andrew Law printed eight chants in his *Rudiments of Music,* 1783, probably because he was teaching at St. Peter's in Philadelphia at the time.) Bull's proposal does raise the question of whether there might have been a demand for this music in Anglican parishes. Both Middletown's Christ Church (now Holy Trinity) and Stratford's Christ Church had small organs in 1756. The former was a gift of Richard Alsop, and the latter was purchased by subscription from Gilbert Deblois, a Boston merchant.[61] Several Church of England parishes had choirs, among them St. John's, North Haven, and St. Mathew's, New Cambridge. Bull's ambitious project apparently languished for lack of subscriptions, for there were no further announcements, and no copies have been located.

Amos Bull's travels in the years preceding his move to New York City, about 1774-75, depict the peripatetic life of a professional singing master. He was rarely in one place long, because a school normally met for a short period of several months. Bull was probably in the New London or New Haven area in 1766, when his proposal appeared in the newspaper. He was still in Wallingford in 1770, where he was involved in land transactions. He was in Middletown in December, 1771, where the First Congregational Church "voted that the Society's Com^tee be Desired to Invite M^r. Amos Bull when he shall Attend Public worship with this Society to Supply S^d. Whitmores [aging Chorister Jacob Whitmore] place in that business."[62] Bull must have declined, for he wrote from New London on January 12, 1772, to his wife's relative in Farmington that, "I shall be ready to begin School with you about ye Middle of February & not sooner if that will not do for you beg you will immediately Inform me. If I hear no more from you on that Head, shall depend on beginning at that time."[63]

Bull's family was already in Farmington, for he wrote, "Desire you will supply my wife with whatever she may want of Cash or Goods & that together with her & Little Lucy, board at your House shall be paid when I come to Farmington . . . ."[64] Bull was back in Middletown in April. His name appears along with those of Nathaniel Shaylor, Oliver Woodward, Mark Dwolf [Deaolph], and William Redfield as choristers for Holy Trinity Church "for yᵉ Year Ensuing."[65] Bull's psalm tune, "Middletown," one of the most frequently printed pieces in American tunebooks, was probably inspired by his residence there.

Bull probably again worked in the New London area before he left for New York. In 1774, the *Connecticut Gazette* advertised, "Just printed and to be sold by T. Green, A new Gamut or Rules of Music: Compiled by Mr. Bull."[66] This was a four-page rudiments of music, the promotional "new" implying that Bull had made some personal amendations to a currently available publication.

Two singing masters from Bolton may also have belonged to the society of the 1769 psalmody meetings in Wallingford and Hartford. They were Oliver Brownson, born May 13, 1746, and Oliver King, born a year later. King published a subscription proposal early in 1775, which confirms their occupations. It is reproduced here in full, not only because it lists a number of other singing masters active in Connecticut, but as it also portrays some of the conditions and methods of tunebook production.

MUSIC

Whereas the Subscriber has for several Years past been employed in teaching Psalmody, and hath found by long Experience that Complaints have generally subsisted amongst the ablest Masters and best Teachers of Music with regard to the Collections of Music that have as yet been made public. In almost every Collection we find a very considerable Part both of Tunes and Anthems, which have not been generally approved of, nor thought worth while to be learned; so that in order to purchase those Tunes that are had in highest Esteem at the present, and probably will continue so, we are put to a greater Expense for the Purchase of those Tunes, and Anthems with them, that are entirely and altogether useless: In order to remedy the above Inconveniency, the Subscriber, at the Advise and Desire of a Number of Gentlemen of the Colony of Connecticut, proposes to Engrave by Subscription.

THE
UNIVERSAL HARMONY,

A Collection of the most choice and Valuable Psalm and Hymn Tunes, Anthems and Canons, with proper Words adapted to the greatest Part, from the most approved Authors, and especially such as have obtained the Approbation of the best Masters in Music: To which will be added, some Pieces which have not yet been published; set by some of the greatest Masters of Music. Also, a plain and easy Explanation of the Rules of Music, fitted for all teachers, learners; and musical Societies.

CONDITIONS

I.   The Book will be printed on fine Paper and the Plates executed by a good Engraver; the whole carefully corrected, set in Score, and the Books well bound.

II. The above Collection will Contain 150 Pages of the same Dimensions as Lyon's Urania.

III. The price to Subscribers will be six Shillings; Lawful Money for each Book.

IV. Any person who shall subscribe for twelve Copies, shall have a Thirteenth *gratis*.

V.   The Money to be paid when the Books are delivered.

Subscriptions are received by Mr. Ingersol, Singing-Master at Lebanon; Mr. Oliver Brunsen, Singing-Master, Litchfield; Mr. Elisha Barber, Simsbury; Mr. Jonathan Benjamin, Singing-Master, Andover; Mr. Bull, Singing Master, New-York; Mr. Charles Deaolph, Singing-Master, Brookline; Mr. Deaolph, Singing-Master, Preston; Mr. Andrew Law, Singing-Master, and Mr. Phillip Paine, Bookseller, Providence; Mr. William McAlpine, and Mr. Andrew Barclay, Bookseller, Boston; at the Printing Office, Norwich; and by the Subscriber at Bolton. Those persons that incline to become Subscribers, are desired to do it as soon as may be, as the Gentlemen who have Subscription Papers in their Hands, will be desired to return them to Messrs. Robertsons and Trumbull, Printers, Norwich, or to the Subscriber in Bolton, by the 20th of April next.

That the Undertakers may know what Encouragement they may have to proceed, the Subscriber will esteem it a Kindness if Gentlemen employed in teaching Music, or any others, will favor him with those tunes and Anthems they may be acquainted with that have not been made public, by sending them to Messers. Robertsons and Trumbull's Printing Office, Norwich, or to the Subscriber at Bolton.

The Public, I trust, will readily see the Advantage of such a Performance, in Point of Usefulness, to any others which have yet been introduced into Practice among us, and also in saving a considerable Sum of Money, annually paid for those Tunes and Anthems that are altogether useless. He has only to observe, that if the Public shall favor this Attempt, he shall always gratefully acknowledge their Kindness, and endeavour to serve them faithfully in his Calling, according to his Capacity, and remains

Their humble Servant,
   OLIVER KING.
Bolton, Feb. 15, 1775.[67]

The date, April 20, for the return of subscriptions to King's collection, tells, in part, why it was probably not published. The skirmish at Lexington on the 19th, and its aftermath, effectively dominated New England's life for a time.

The production of American tunebooks, which began with *Urania* in 1761, has been recognized as a logical outgrowth of a widespread musical education given largely in singing schools.[68] Even those fortunate to be able to attend college usually arrived with singing school experience. Both Andrew Law (Brown, 1775) and Benjamin Trumbull (Yale, 1759), for example, taught music throughout their college years. Trumbull kept accounts of "money receiv'd for writing and scholling in New Haven in the year 1758":

For a singing book Sold to Goodwin 8s
For making a singing book for Sherwin 2/6
              one for White 6/6
              one for Gilbert 7/0
. . . rec'd of Samuel Whiting 8s for tuition[69]

Yale College students contributed music theses, listed under *Theses Physicae*, every year, excepting four, between 1755 and 1774.

Singing masters may have concerned themselves with physics of sound, but in the course of keeping school, their concentration was on practical learning. Lessons began with rudiments of music, note-reading, and vocal technique and progressed to learning and practicing choral music. The psalmody repertory had expanded by the seventies, especially in the years after Lyon's *Urania* and Billings' *The New-England Psalm-Singer* (Boston, 1770) were published. Although a larger selection of printed music collections containing a wider variety of vocal forms were available for teachers' use and students' purchase, it would be safe to say that many more students made up their own music books from blank paper sewn between heavy paper covers than were able to purchase one of the printed collections from either England or America. In addition, the stability of the traditional psalm tunes in their plain harmonized versions, as the basic musical material for instruction, is evident in the contents of commonplace books filled with music by a number of Connecticut students.[70]

Captain Samuel Whitman of West Hartford compiled a typical collection which included psalm tunes, the popular "Morning, Evening, and Cradle Hymns," "An Elegy made on ye Death of Queen Mary," "The Gliding Streams," and the perennial favorites, "Pompey's Ghost" (text only) and "Advice to the Fair Sex." Whitman copied the bass and tenor parts for most of his choices, using the old C clef for the tenor.[71] Susanna Miles copied treble and tenor parts, both on G clefs, for the psalm tunes in her music book. Each student wrote out the tune (usually in the tenor) and the part he or she needed, which made each book a part book in the traditional fashion.

Sometime in the 1750s or 1760s a new and inexpensive teaching aid for the singing master was developed. A pamphlet of three, then

From Samuel Whitman, His Book, 1768

four almanac-size pages containing rudiments of music, *The Gamut, or Scale of Musick* may have been a Connecticut invention. The idea caught on, since issues with blank staves on the back pages continued to be published into the nineteenth century. Newspaper advertisements for *The Gamut* did not appear outside of Connecticut prior to the 1790s, and earlier issues that have come to light are bound in manuscript commonplace books filled with music copied by Connecticut residents. An early example is bound in Susanna Miles' singing book.[72] A different watermark appears on *The Gamut* pages than on the stock which makes up the rest of the book. This single fold, inserted between the first and second manuscript-filled pages, forms two conjugate leaves, of which page [1] is *The Gamut,* page [2] the "Rules for finding mi," and page [3] the "Musical Characters." It was similar to a slip ballad sheet, or single column sheet, popular for selling half-penny ballads in the eighteenth century.[73] *The Gamut* could be mass-produced cheaply, and sold at very little price. In 1788, Nathaniel Patten advertised *The Gamut* at 4d singly and 3s a dozen.[74]

Samuel Whitman's music book contains a copy of a later four-page issue of *The Gamut.* "The Rule of Proportion of Notes, or Length of Time in Musick" is printed on page 4. Enodias Bidwell of East Hartford had the same *Gamut* version in his music book (1772).[75] *The Gamut* also employed a traditional education device: clever verses to aid learning. The verse on the "Musical Characters" page of Samuel Whitman's *Gamut,* for example, is inspired by an almost identical verse in the introduction to John Arnold's *Church Music Reformed* (London, 1765).

> Unless these Notes, Names, Marks
> are perfect learnt by Heart,
> None ever will attain to Musick's
> pleasant Art.

The indebtedness of American teachers and compilers to British musicians and theoreticians took many forms.

Both the three and four-"page" *Gamut* were printed before musical type was widely available in America. For the "Musical Characters," only the text was printed, and the lines and characters had to be added by hand. In the *Gamut,* the "cliff" signs and lines had also to be drawn by hand. A *Gamut* edition from the post-war period, pasted in the front of Jesse Rogers's music manuscript, has the same four pages, but the clef signs, staff lines, and the "Musical Characters" are printed.[76]

Music education also took place under auspices other than those of the specialized singing schools. Instrumental tutors, the *Gamut,* and music books of all kinds were available for self-instruction and for music making at home. Yale College and private schools included

THE
G A M U T,
OR
SCALE OF MUSICK.

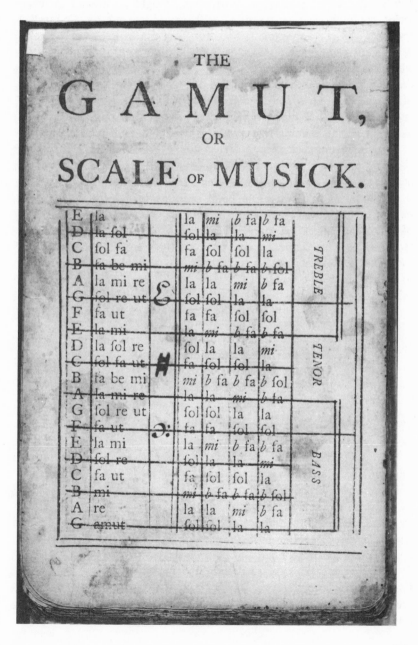

music in their curricula. Isaac Bull in Litchfield advertised for pupils in 1765, and offered "Spelling, Reading, Writing, Cyphering, and the Rules of Music."[77] At Moor's Indian Charity School in Lebanon Crank, proficiency in psalmody was a required skill, especially for older students being prepared for missionary work. The Reverend Eleazar Wheelock, who began teaching boys from Indian tribes in his home, moved to the new school building in 1755, and by 1765, had increased the number of charity scholars to 10 girls, 29 boys, and 7 white students.[78] Wheelock (Yale, 1733) presumably received at least a part of his musical training under Rector Elisha Williams, a Regular-singing enthusiast. During the Great Awakening, Wheelock established personal relationships with English dissenters, such as Watts, Whitefield, and Wesley, and shared their views about music's role in congregational worship.

In 1765, Wheelock sent his prize graduate, Samson Occom, with Nathaniel Whitaker, of Norwich, to England to solicit funds for the school. English singing master and compiler Thomas Knibb met them both, and sent a number of his collections to the school in a shipment of books assembled by agent Robert Keen. Occom's musical training is attested to in a letter Knibb sent to Occom during his stay there. He wrote:

> Rev[d]. S[r]
> understanding by the Rev[d]. Dr. Whitaker that you know Music I here Present you with upwards of Six score Tunes amongst which there are several of the Moder[n]est & some of the Pleasantest that are us[d]. amongst the Methodists & if at any time it should suit your conveniancy to call & Drink a Dish of Tea at my House should be glad to sing a few of them over together & D[r] Whitaker assist the Band
> > from S[r] your
> > Humble Servant
> > Tho[s]. Knibb
> Bishopsgate Street N[o] 90
> > near Spital Square
> > Feb[r]. y[e] 8th. 1768[79]

Occom's own *Collection of Hymns and Spiritual Songs* was published in New London in 1774.

The accomplishments of the students and graduates of Wheelock's school testify to their musical training, which included instructions in notereading and choral singing. A Boston merchant, John Smith, made a special visit to the school in May of 1764, and he reported that he was "movingly touched on giveing out the Psalm to hear an Indian youth set the Line and the others following him, and singing the tenor, and base, with remarkable gravity and seriousness. . . ."[80]

Wheelock sent his graduates into the field prepared to teach singing schools as part of their Christianizing mission. He outfitted David Fowler, a Montauk Indian and brother-in-law of Samson Occom, as follows:

David Fowler has rec[d] a pr. of shoes 8/ a Dowlass Shirt Stick of Silk and Hair black silk stock: another White Cotten's M[r]. Lyon's Urania 11/8. Setts of his Journey with my Horse to Mount Johnson [New York] June 29th, 1762. The Lord make his way prosperous and direct in the whole of the Business he is going upon.[81]

Urania was available to the public in June of 1762, according to Oscar Sonneck, but Wheelock may have purchased copies earlier when they became available to subscribers (1761). At any rate, Fowler could not have been equipped with a more "modern" music collection to use in his work. He wrote to Wheelock in 1765,

This is the twelfth Day since I began to keep this School and I have put eight of my [26] scholars into the third page of their Spelling-book . . . . I am also teaching a Singing-School. They take great pleasure in learning to Sing. We can already carry three Parts of several Tunes.[82]

Samuel Kirkland, a non-Indian student at the school for two years, wrote to Wheelock from New York, that he "kept a Singing-School every Night in the Week except Saturday-night."[83] Wheelock enthused to the Reverend Nathaniel Whitaker:

[Kirkland's students] have made a great Proficiency in the Schools in Reading & Singing—of the latter he says, he hears no such Singing in the Country,—they carry three parts with great exactness—and many of them yet eager to improve further in the Art—This is all new, and beyond what was ever yet known among Indians—Many of them Say, they never knew Such Pleasure before—That it is worth while to be Christians, if they had nothing more by it, than the Pleasure of Singing Praises to God—And to assist them further Mr. Kirkland has already begun, & designs to go on, to translate Psalms & Sacred Hymns into their Language, and fit them to Tunes—This is Surprising and affecting to some, that come among them from foreign Tribes—[84]

The best description of music teaching by Wheelock's Indian students is provided by Mohegan Joseph Johnson, at work among the Tunxis Indians in Farmington. Extracts from his journal speak for themselves.

Fryday the 27th of November AD 1772
    kept School as Usual, at Evening held a Meeting at the house of Samuel Adams, a Singing Meeting. At the close we Concluded to have the singing Meeting twice in a week, that is, Tuesday night,

and Fryday night, also we agreed further to spend some time for Publick worship, together, and we appointed, and set apart, the Sabbath Evenings for that purpose, that is to Sing, pray, and give a word of Exhortation or spend some part of it in Reading some book of Edification.

Saturday, the 28th of November AD 1772
kept the school in the forepart of the day, in the after part, went over to the town, got paper . . .
Thursday the 3d day of December AD 1772
This morning after we had tended family worship, I made 3 gamuts, or Singing Books. That is, Cut them out, & sewed them together. I began to write down the rules in one. The indians are all desirous of having Gamuts, but I am in Continual hurry. nevertheless I purpose to furnish them with Singing books as soon as time will admit. I just dismissed my scholars who was very regular the day past, and several seem to be in Earnest to learn . . .

Fryday the 4th Day of December AD 1772
[Evening at friends] . . . heard his daughters sing several Tunes— and sang some at there desire, myself. very pleasant Evening—. . . before school I wrote down the Musical Characters—[singing meeting in the evening] . . .

Saturday the 5th Day of December AD 1772
very pleasant. rose very early, wrote considerable before school, in my Gamut, the first part . . .
. . . spent chief of this afternoon in writing. and in Drawing lines, for my Gamut . . . [went to the house of his landlord Wodsworth] & delivered him his Singing Book . . .

Monday the 7th of December AD 1772
Began to prick out some tunes in my Gamut . . .

Tuesday the 8th of December AD 1772
Still prick't out more tunes . . .

Wednesday the 9th
Prick't out as usual . . .

. . .

Windsday 27th [January], 1773
Finished Susannah's Gamut. The Eighth Gamut I made.

[Johnson notes on January 30th that he has kept school 10 weeks.]
. . . My Challenge is that they excell this tribe in Singing. The Musical Art. if your tribes can attend that part of solemn worship with Deacency . . . .[85]

A logical consequence of all the music education going on was the "choir movement" in Connecticut churches. These trained singers, music specialists, naturally wanted to sit together in order to perform the more complex three and four-part anthems and fuging pieces that became fashionable. In Woodstock, Isaac Bowen and Elias Mason petitioned the First Society for seats in the gallery in order to relieve the "Inconveniences . . . of those who Joyn with us in Singing being separated from one another in the Congregation whereby Discord often Ensues . . . ."[86] The Society responded with a vote that they "would be exceedingly glad that the three forward Seats in the front gallery might be Sequestered principally to the use of the Singers and would take it quite kindly if people would—accordingly conform there to."[87] People apparently did not wish to comply, for another vote was needed five years later, which stated clearly that gallery seats were to be "devoted" to the singers.[88]

Placement of singers around three sides of the gallery created a spatial musical effect which impressed John Adams when he visited Middletown's Congregational Church in 1771:

> Heard the finest Singing, that ever I heard in my Life, the front and side Galleries were crowded with Rows of Lads and Lasses, who performed all the Parts in the Utmost Perfection. *I thought I was wrapped up.* A Row of Women all standing up, and playing their Parts with perfect Skill and Judgment, added a Sweetness and Sprightliness to the whole which absolutely charmed me.[89]

The sound environment in church buildings where the choir sang from positions along the front and sides of the gallery, as pictured on the title page of Oliver Brownson's *Select Harmony,* was ideally suited to the musical structure of fuging tunes, as well as plain three and four-part psalm tunes with spare harmony and open chords. American psalmodists have often being faulted for "primitive" harmonic practices, but they knew what they liked. It is reasonable to believe that composers designed their music to suit the special effects that could be achieved with the gallery arrangement in buildings with plain surfaces and few curtains and carpets. The popularity of the fuging tune (successive vocal entries and overlapping text sections), which American, and especially Connecticut composers, developed into a versatile genre, must certainly be attributed in part to these special effects created by the physical spaces in which they were performed.

Experiments in procedure and repertory were frequently made in the afternoon service or in the mid-week lecture service, before they were attempted in Sunday morning worship. Lining-out the psalm was dispensed with for the afternoon service in East Hartford, at the same time (1772) its singers were placed in the front and side gallery seats.[90] In 1774, Litchfield's First Society changed a number of practices all at once when they voted to introduce Mr. [Eliphalet?] Lyman's method of singing into Sunday worship, give his singers sole use of the front gallery seats, and pay him 30/ per month for four months or as long as he kept school. The pastor, Judah Champion, was empowered to begin worship with singing, and without "Lineal Reading."[91] Committees were instructed to select new music in some churches, such as Middletown's Congregational Church, where a 26-man study group was directed to examine trends elsewhere and "from time to time Choose and appoint Such tunes to be used & Introduced into Publick worship."[92]

White Haven Church in New Haven appointed Deacon Lyman and the chorister to "draw up a list of tunes," totalling thirty.

> The ch[h] also at the same time empowered the same committee to arrange the s[d] thirty tunes into proper order under six distinct heads or classes, & voted y[t] those tunes be sung hereafter generally in y[t] order, five on a sabbath for six sabbaths, & than to begin again: & so on in continued rotation.[93]

Complaints that there were too many new tunes, especially for the "elderly people" led to a reduction of authorized tunes to a total of twenty-five, but "progress" went forward with a vote for "singing without reading," a practice "w[h] obtains in so many other places."[94]

North Haven's Congregational Church kept pace with the times by agreeing ". . . some times to use D[r]. Watt's Hymns in the Worship of God, when they are better suited to the Subject, and more for Edification than any particular Psalms."[95] A comprehensive plan for congregational music was prepared by the pastor, Benjamin Trumbull. Not all congregations were fortunate in having so well-organized a leader. Trumbull recommended a choice of tunes that were "the most Plain and Least Difficult to be Sung," and no more than 2 or 3 new tunes in Common Meter, 1 in Long Meter, and possibly 2 in Short Meter be introduced to replace others discarded. A Society committee would attend the "singing meetings" and agree on new tunes and their time of introduction. Trumbull's education plan made provision both for training in note reading, rudiments of music, and choral singing, and for learning music by ear for those who did not desire to become music specialists.

> It is proposed that Such as Desire to Learn to Sing by Rule and will Steadily attend & make themselves in any Good measure Masters of it shall be instructed & have such Books as are Necessary for the Purpose gratis, Provided they find the Paper for the Books, and Shall be instructed at Such Times and Places as they shall from Time to Time agree to.—With regard to others who only chuse to learn by Rote, if they will attend after a Number of those above Mentioned have well learnt a Tune, they shall Meet at the Meeting House and there Sing Psalms and Hymns that others may have the opportunity to Learn them; . . ."[96]

Trumbull concluded that the congregation would "be able to keep time well, which is a great Excellency in Psalmody and without which there can be no harmony in Singing." A *Courant* front-page story, possibly an editorial, about a misbehaving singing school student who came to see the "propriety of beating time in singing which many make a ridicule of . . ."[97] points up the centrality of the issue of "keeping time well." The complaints were still coming from conservatives and Old-way singers, probably aimed at the chorister and his singers (visibly keeping time) in the gallery. Some of the issues which concerned musical reformers in the 1720s were still current in the 1770s, and some of the same arguments for progress in choral singing appeared in a *Courant* editorial of September 14, 1773. The pace of change was never even in every corner of the colony.

New procedures and practices were the rule, not only in worship, but also in military service. For one thing, the training manual in use, Bland's Exercise, was now, according to the General Assembly, "prolix and incumbered with many useless motions," and therefore, the militia would for the future train under the Norfolk Militia Exercise.[98] The instruments that regulated daily military routine, both in training maneuvers and on active duty with the British Army, were the drum and trumpet. As Isaac Stiles said in a sermon on the occasion of the departure of Captain Nathan Whiting's company from New Haven,

> . . . a Soldier ought to understand the Words of Command; the several Beats of that great warlike Instrument the Drum, together with the Language of the shrill high-sounding Trumpet. . . .[99]

A new element was added about mid-century with the reintroduction of the fife into the British Army. Drum beatings were thereafter accompanied by a melodic counterpart played by the fife.[100] The training manual did not spell out the musical signals, so they were learned from the drum and fife majors or by self-instruction.[101] About the time of the Boston massacre, a young man wrote in his journal, "I was so fond of hearing the fife and drum played by the British that somehow or other I got possession of an old split fife, and having made it sound by puttying up the crack, learned to play several tunes upon it sufficiently well to be fifer in the militia company of Captain Gay."[102] The order of procession for the coronation of George III reported in New Haven, emphasizes the renewed importance of the fife in military music:

3 A Fife in a Livery Coat of Scarlet richly laced
4 Four Drums cloathed as the Fife
5 The Drum-Major
6 Eight Trumpeters, four a-breast, in rich Liveries of Crimson Velvet
7 Kettle Drums, with Banners of Crimson Damask

8 Eight Trumpeters as before, four a-breast
9 The Serjeant-Trumpeter

. . .

25 Children of the Choir at Westminster

. . .

27 Children of the Chappel Royal
28 Choir of Westminster, two and two
29 Organ Blower and groom of the Vestry
30 Three of his Majesty's Musicians
31 Gentlemen of the Chappel Royal[103]

The British Army regimental bands exerted a durable influence in the colonies, both by their military and non-military performances. A typical example of the latter was the commencement in Philadelphia, reported in the *Connecticut Gazette* in 1767:

> . . . an ode set to music was sung by Master Bankson . . . accompanied by the organ, &c. under the conduct of a worthy son of the college, . . . The band belonging to the 18th, or royal regiment of Ireland, was kindly permitted, by the colonel, to perform in the instrumental part.[104]

A band of music usually had a minimum of eight players: two clarinets, two oboes, two French horns, and two bassons. Wind players frequently doubled on string instruments. John Smith, for example, was a "private soldier and Musicianer" who deserted the British 44th Regiment of Foot at Crown Point. He played "extraordinary well on the Bassoon, and likewise on the Violen," according to his commanding officers.[105] A band's repertory would have included overtures, such as those of composers Gossec, Stamitz, or Handel, concertos or solos, pieces from operas, theater songs, dance music, and concerted chamber pieces. Bands performed for the entertainment of the officers who supported them, in addition to their service on military and public ceremonial occasions.

The field music, on the other hand, whether drums and fifes or drums and trumpets, were responsible for the everyday work routine in camp. Drum majors instructed drummers in the duty based upon traditional practices, learned in the British army or in militia training units. "The music that the trumpeters played, usually accompanied by tonic-dominant tones in the kettle drums," according to Raoul Camus, "consisted primarily of fanfares and flourishes."[106] Melodies for the fife came from many sources, including theater music, popular songs, dance tunes, and folk ballads. A tune often wore a number of guises, depending on whether it was an air sung between acts of a play, a concert song, a fiddle dance accompaniment, or an instrumental march. A good example is the song "British Grenadiers," which Josiah Flagg programmed for a Boston concert, the "vocal part to be performed by four voices, and to conclude with the British Grenadiers."[107]

The tune is descended from "All You that Love Good Fellows," to which the old ballad "The Honour of a London Prentice" was set.[108] It was reprinted in *Wit and Mirth: or Pills to Purge Melancholy,* edited by Thomas D'Urfey. A text published in London during the French and Indian war, "Some boast of Alexander and some of Hercules," appeared on a broadside printed in New London about 1760, with phrases altered and two verses interpolated.[109] The process of song-text composition can be illustrated by comparing the first two verses.

London Text

Some talk of Alexander & some of
    Hercules,
Of Conon & Lysander & some Meltiadies
But of all the World's brave Heroes
    there's none that can compare,
With a tow row row row row to the
    British Granadiers.
None of those ancient Heroes e'er saw a
    CannonBal,
Or knew the Force of Powder to flay their
    Foes w^t. all,
But our brave Boys do know it & banish
    all their Fears,
With a tow, row, row, row, row, the
    British GRANADIERS.[110]

New London Text

Some boast of Alexander and some of
    Hercules,
Of Hector and Lysander and such
    folks as these,
That all the world acknowledges true
    Courage doth appear,
With a foll doll doll toll toll,—the
    British Grenadier.
Those Fops that are call'd Heroes ne'er
    saw a cannon Ball
Nor knew the Force of Powder to drive
    their Foes withal,
But we bolder Boys that know it do
    banish all Fear,
With foll doll doll, toll, loll,—the
    British Grenadier.[111]

A third text, written in the "Orderly Book of Captn Thomas Hamelton Company" of Pennsylvania's 3rd Regiment, exhibits orally transmitted text variants which resulted when the writer set down the verses as he heard them, or as he may have remembered them.

Some talks of Alexander
& Some of Harkelass
Some talks of Cananading
& Some of Marchindise
But of all yᵉ world Brave Heroes
There is few yᵗ Can Compare
to be hold with admeration
the British Granadears—[112]

The "British Grenadiers" was the tune designated for a "Song on Liberty," printed in the *Courant* at the beginning of the Revolution; Giles Gibbs wrote out his version in his music book as "The British Grenadiers March."[113] The tune appeared with the text "some talk of Alexander" on the London broadside.[114]

BRITISH GRENADIERS

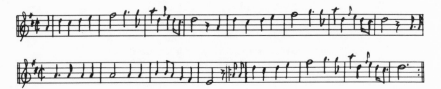

In many ways, **Connecticut** colonists were preparing musically for events that followed. Two years before Lexington, the *Courant* carried an advertisement stating that

As a Military Spirit seems to be recovering in this Colony, this is to give Notice to all Gentlemen Officers, that they may be supply'd with DRUMS, By John Rogers, of Middletown, equally for Sound, and neatness of Work to any that can be bought in Boston or New York and painted equal to any, if desired by his employers.[115]

The motto painted on his drums by Mr. Rogers may well have been *"qui transtulit sustinet,"* or "God, who transplanted us hither, will support us."[116]

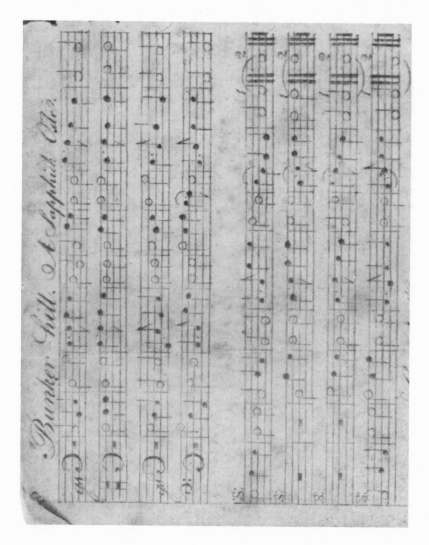

Music in the War Years

Boston to Yorktown

Why should vain Mortals tremble at the Sight of
Death and Destruction in The Field of Battle,
Where Blood and Carnage clothe the Ground in Crimson,
Sounding with Death-Groans? . . .

Life, for my Country and the Cause of Freedom,
Is but a Trifle for a Worm to part with;
And if preserved in so great a Contest,
Life is redoubled.

From *The American Hero*, by Nathaniel Niles.[1]

O N Wednesday, April 19, 1775, the first military action of the Revolutionary War took place, and within four days the news had traversed the length of Connecticut via post rider.[2] The response to the Lexington alarm was immediate, for "in town after town, militiamen organized and marched off to Boston. Archival records . . . list some 3,600 men from nearly fifty towns . . . ."[3] In New Haven, Yale students joined the militia for maneuvers on the Green. Freshman Noah Webster, so his biographer reports, paced the drill with his flute.[4] Senior Ebenezer Huntington, who later commanded Webb's Additional Regiment, marched to Boston as a volunteer with the New Haven militia.[5] Benedict Arnold's elite New Haven Guards (later the Second Company of The Governor's Foot Guard) served 28 days, as did the Windham militia, the longest service recorded in the Lexington alarm.[6]

With the militia units marched their fifers and drummers. More than 50 musicians are listed on the Lexington rolls, 41 by name:

NAME	POSITION	SERVICE	TOWN
Allen, John	Fifer	22 Days	Colchester
Burnham, Gurdon	Drum'r	10	Hartford
Butler, Asa	Fifer	2	Stafford
Case, Nehemiah	Drum^r	3	Coventry
Chapman, Oliver	Fifer	?	East Windsor
Converse, Jude	Drummer	9	Stafford
Eastman, Peter	Drum'r	10	Ashford
Flyn, John	Trumpeter	13	Woodstock
Fosdick, William	Fifer	6	Wethersfield
Foster, Chauncey	Fifer	?	East Windsor
Gilbert, Ebenezer, Junr	Fifer	21	Hebron

Gillet, Nathan	Fifer	1	Simsbury
Hale, Samuel	Drum^r	9	Suffield
Hanks, Benjamin	Drum'r	27	Mansfield
Hibbard, David, Junr	Drum^r	3	Coventry
Hollister, David	Drum'r	4	Glastonbury
Howlet, William	Drum^r	13	Woodstock
Jennings, Jonathan, Junr	Fifer	28	Windham
King, Charles, Junr	Fifer	21	Bolton
Loomiss, Abner	Drummer	6	Bolton
Lothrop, Abner	Drum'r	28	Windham
McMullen, Daniel	Fifer	7	Wallingford
Mead, John 3^d	Drum'r	6	Greenwich
Merriam, Ephraim	Fifer	7	Wallingford
Nye, David	Fifer	4	Glastonbury
Olmstead, Timothy	Fifer	4	Hartford
Pall, John	Fifer	6	Greenwich
Pease, Aaron	Drum'r	26	Enfield
Pinney, Lemuel	Fifer	5	East Windsor
Russell, Stephen	Drum^r	?	East Windsor
Steel, Stephen, Junr	Fifer	7	Tolland
Strong, Roger	Fifer	23	Lebanon
Treat, Jonathan	Drum'r	4	Glastonbury
Tryon, William	Drum^r	6	Wethersfield
Tyler, Nathaniel	Drum'r	18	Canterbury
Waldo, Cornelius	Drum'r	8	Canterbury
Warner, Stephen	Drum^r	?	East Windsor
Washburn, Moses	Drum^r	2	Stafford
Watson, John, Junr	Fifer	19	Pomfret
Whipple, Noah	Fifer	12	Tolland
Willcox, Asa	Private (Drummer)	3	New Hartford
Wilson, John	Drum'r	18	Killingly
[Captain Comfort Sage, Troop of Horse]	2 Trumpeters	5 each	Middletown
[Captain Return J. Meigs, Light Infantry]	1 Fifer, 1 Drummer	8 each	Middletown
[Benedict Arnold's Guards]	1 Fifer, 1 Drummer	28 each	New Haven
[Captain John Ely]	1 Drummer	5	Saybrook[7]

The fifers, trumpeters, and drummers who marched to Lexington knew the camp duty from their militia training. The activities of the daily routine, from going for water and wood to accompanying prisoners, were signalled by the drummers. Time-keeping functions were especially crucial. For example, general orders of April 26 directed

> That the Revaley Beat Every Morning at 4 o clock That the Beating of the Troop the officers and picquit [guard] be Immeadatly Assembled on the parade. The Tatoe to Beat Every Evening at Nine o clock That after yᵉ Beating of the Tatoo there Be a profound Silence through the camp.[8]

The drum beatings were accompanied by melodies played on the fife. Since the militia units at Lexington came from several colonies and had, as a consequence, trained under different manuals, these duty signals were not uniform.

The first few months in camp around Boston must have been fraught with many problems stemming from disparities in soldiers' preparedness. General Israel Putnam's regimental orders for June 24, 1775, reflected the need to bring order into camp routine. They stated

> That Every officer and soldier under My Command and Capt Coits and those officers and soldiers in his Company all Belonging to and Raised in the Colony of Connecticut are ordered on Every ocation when the Drums Beat to arms Immediatly to Repaire to the Parade near the Incampment Laid out for my Regiment and there form themselves and wait for Further oders and it is Further ordered that all the Drums and Fifes in the Regmᵗ Do there Duty at the proper houres according to the Rules of there Duty in the Camp.[9]

These "Rules" were communicated to the musicians by specially selected drum and fife majors, who were responsible as well for training both practicing musicians and new recruits. Lieutenant Abraham Chittenden noted in his journal how ". . . the Drums and Fifes [were] to be on yᵉ Parade at 9 o Clock where . . . [the officers would] look out the neatest person for Drum and Fife major."[10] At Boston, the General Orders, July 1, 1775, stated that "the Drummers in Camps attend on Mʳ John Bassett Drum Majʳ at 7 o clock to Morrow allso Recᵛ there orders Respeting thre Duty."[11] Fifers would have responded to that directive along with the drummers; the term "drums" often meant all the field music.

On July 3, George Washington, newly-appointed Commander-in-Chief of the new Continental Army, took command of the forces around Boston. His journey from Philadelphia to Massachusetts was attended from town to town by escorts of local militia. In New Haven he took time to review the military company of Yale College. Noah Webster liked to relate in later years how he played his flute for the Yale students as they escorted General Washington's party out from New Haven as far as Neckbridge.[12]

After Washington arrived in Boston, he faced the major task of organizing a "loose aggregation of men" into an army "patterned on European models."[13] His first weeks' orders were aimed at correcting obvious problems.

> [July 8, 1775] It is ordered that the Main Guard on no account Whatever be without a Drum which is to beat to arms on any Alarm and Followed by all the Drums in the Camp on which Every Officer & Soldier is Immeadiatly to Repair to the alarm post.[14]

On July 20, Washington observed that

> Certain Drums in or near Cambridge very improperly beat the Revilee this morning before Day, altho the troops are ordered to be under arms half and hour before daylight. It is not supposed that the Revilee is to be beat at that time for the Revilee is not to be beat untill the Sentinels can Distinguish a Person 1000 yards around them clearly.[15]

Reveille carried a twofold meaning (see page 72): soldiers were to prepare for the duties of the day, and the sentries were to cease challenging. Proper signaling was obviously fundamental to a well-run camp.

Because their preparatory military training had not been standardized, inevitable confusion in operations prevailed within the gathering of men from all over New England. At the same time, this was undoubtedly the first opportunity for many small-town militiamen to travel and to exchange experiences with their counterparts from other colonies. The musicians who arrived in Boston already equipped with the basic skills would, most certainly, have indulged in a favorite pastime of fifers: namely, tune-swapping. Besides informal communication, musicians were automatically subject to the influence of their official instructors. The Norfolk Exercise, under which Connecticut militia units trained until the General Assembly ordered a change (December, 1775), did not spell out musical signals. These were transmitted by the fife and drum majors. An aspiring musician could also follow a printed "tutor" to teach himself. At camp near Boston, instruction was part of prescribed routine, and at the end of July, Washington stressed its perennial need by issuing an order reiterating the requirement. "The Drumers and Fifers of the Regm[ts] in and about Cambridge are Constantly to attend the Drum and Fife Maj[rs] at the Usual hours of Instruction."[16]

Stabilization of the repertory was imperative following the reintroduction of the fife and the addition of its melodic counterpart to the drum beating signals. An example of one of the duty calls is "The

Drummers Call," which assembled musicians to perform their tasks. The tune appears in most fife tutors and on one of the first pages in several extant fife manuscripts.

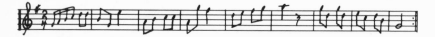

Another duty call was the "Tattoo," which marked the end of a day's work. The word "tatoo" came from the word "tap-too," literally to turn off the taps of innkeeper's casks, and meant the close of business for the day.[17]

The "Retreat," an ancient ceremony when roll was called and orders for the next day read, "has vestiges of the period of the medieval walled towns. At the completion of the beating of Retreat by the drummers around the city walls or in the open fields just before them, the gates were shut, the drawbridge raised, the city sealed until the following morning at the beating of the Reveille."[18] Chaplain Ammi Robbins, with Colonel Burrall's Litchfield Regiment in the northern campaign of 1776, described his part in the retreat.

> [September 4] At night prayed and sang with the brigade. This exercise is often held on the parade ground, when the music march up and the drummers lay their drums in a very neat style in two rows, one above the other; it always takes five, and often the rows are very long; occasionally they make a platform for me to stand upon and raise their drums a number of tier.[19]

Robbins later wrote, "Monday, 30 . . . Prayed at night with the brigade. Sometimes Tibbals, who strikes the drum admirably, gives it a touch at the right time when we are singing—it is beautiful harmony. A soft fife is also an addition."[20] The melody could have been "Lovely Nancy," a song from the opera *The Jovial Crew* (London, 1731).[21] The tune, titled "Lovely Nancy A Retreat" in contemporary fife manuscripts and absent from British tutors, may have had a specific American usage.[22]

A variety of literature provided the sources for tunes adopted for military use. In many cases, the melodies were part of a repertory shared with popular song and dance traditions. Good examples are "The Flowers of Edinburgh"[23] and "Over the Hills and Far Away."[24] Some melodies came from composers' stage works or choral pieces; George F. Handel's *Occasional Oratorio* (London, 1746) was the source for a march known as "General Wolfe's March."[25]

The same repertory also provided clock-makers with the tunes they incorporated in the music-box type of mechanism of their chime clocks. Hoopes pointed out that "no two have the same set of tunes, from which it may be inferred that the melodies were selected by the pur-

From Giles Gibbs' Music Book

chasers."[26] These musical clocks, many still in working order, represent an overlooked indicator of popular taste. One famous Connecticut clock, formerly in the Hanks family, now stands in the John Quincy Adams state drawing room in the State Department Building in Washington. It was made for Uriah Hanks of Mansfield in 1776, during his son Benjamin's apprenticeship with Thomas Harland of Norwich.[27] Its six tunes are "Lass of Pattys Mill," "Shady Bowers," "Minuet by Handel," "Lovely Nymph," "Ms. Hales Minuet," and "Psalm Tune."

Clock-maker Daniel Burnap, born in Coventry November 1, 1759, reputedly played the fife at age 14 with his father, Captain Abraham's, militia company. Hoopes suggests that "Burnap's boyhood experience as a fifer would have given him the necessary familiarity with written music to make its transfer to the pin barrel of a chime clock an easy task,"[28] or Burnap could, of course, have learned the tunes by ear. Some of the tunes Burnap used are "Air by Handel," "Banks of the Dee," "A Lovely Lass," "Lovely Nymph" (published in *The Select Songster*), a "Minuit by T. Olmsted" (Connecticut musician and composer), "Maid of the Mill," and dance tunes such as "Successful Campaign" and "Dutchess of Brunswick."[29] Peregrine White used marches, dances, and Psalm 149 for his chime clocks.[30] Militiaman Calvin Pease, obviously impressed with a chime clock he saw on the way to Boston, wrote in his journal, "we staid at Captain bornam that night I see a Clock that would play tunes With 10 hammers . . . ."[31]

Many tunes were simply copied from printed British collections. *The Compleat Tutor for the Fife* (London, Thompson and Sons, c. 1759) appears to be Gibbs' source for many of his melodies.[32] For example, when he copied "The Marquis of Granby's March," Gibbs began with the sixth measure. Noticing his mistake only after he had copied three more melodies, he recopied the entire tune on the next available page. The only fife tutor thus far located in which the tune is laid out in the same way is the Thompson collection. An American printing of an English tutor was probably available after 1776, but it is known only through Michael Hillegas's advertisement in the *Pennsylvania Gazette*. The work was supposed to include "beside the fife duty, and the usual collection of lessons airs [and] marches in the English edition, a variety of new favourite ones never before printed."[33] The "new favourite ones" probably comprised the last four pages of the book, which are reproduced in a later edition published by Willig (1805), and include "Lovely Nancy" and "Yankee Doodle."[34]

The musicians in military service were responsible not only for signals, transmitting orders and commands, but also for attendance at ceremonies and other occasions for which the entire encampment would assemble. The administration of disciplinary action, frequently lashing and dismissal, was a public business, and the field music played a

DANIEL BURNAP'S CLOCK

Courtesy of The Connecticut Historical Society

prominent part. Ensign Nathaniel Morgan saw "one of the rif [le] men whipped 39 stripes and . . . drummed out of the camps [by] 55 drummers and 60 fifers."[35] Simeon Lyman of Sharon and drummer Calvin Pease both described a scene two days earlier in which "a man . . . was whipped 39 lashes and then drummed out of the camp with 16 drums and 8 fifes."[36] The music traditionally played for this purpose was "The Rogues March," found in most printed fife tutors and manuscript fife books. Civilians often received the same treatment. A soldier's wife, caught stealing a garment, was dealt with by Colonel Israel Angell, who wrote, "I took the Gound in order to Send it to the owner and ordered all the Drums and fifes to parade and Drum her out of the Reg^t. with a paper pind to her back, with these words in Cappital letters, [A THIEF] thus She went off with Musick—."[37]

Funeral ceremonies for soldiers and civilians were similar in formal arrangements and in their music. The military procession was accompanied by a "dead march," for which several melodies sufficed. Chaplain Ammi Robbins observed, "There is something more than ordinarily solemn and touching in our funerals, especially an officer's; swords and arms inverted, others with their arms folded across their breast stepping slowly to the *beat* of the muffled drum."[38] Benjamin Boardman, chaplain of the Second Connecticut Regiment at Boston, noted that for Lieutenant Wadsworth's funeral ". . . on the fife was played the tune called Funeral Thoughts. At the end of each line in the tune the drums beat one stroke."[39] "Funeral Thoughts," commonly sung for civilian funerals, is attributed to English composer Aaron Williams, whose *Universal Psalmodist* (1763) was a model for American psalmodists. The text most often used was Isaac Watts's hymn, "Hark from the Tombs a doleful sound." The ceremonies for the Reverend Dr. Napthali Daggett, Professor of Divinity at Yale College, "closed by singing the funeral thought."[40] Gibbs copied out the melody on the same page with two dance tunes.

"Roslin Castle," another melody played for the dead march, was printed in the *Caledonian Pocket Companion,* where it is called "Roselana Castle."[41] According to legend, the tune was played by Scottish bagpipers stationed in New York in honor of the castle at Roslyn. Music and text were printed in the *Boston Magazine* in 1783.[42] Fife major Nathaniel Brown, from Durham, wrote out "The Rosling Castle —Dead March" for two fifes in his manuscript (1781). The facsimile, with the same variant title, is from Fife Major Aaron Thompson's journal and music book.

Attendance at Sabbath worship was required of all soldiers, when circumstances permitted. Chaplain Ammi Robbins held evening meetings as well, like those that became standard practice among New Light preachers, such as Wheelock and Pomeroy. Robbins apparently intended

to incorporate features of singing meetings such as those Joseph Johnson described in his Farmington diary. Robbins noted, "I proposed to amend and reform the singing which had a good effect. Prayed, sang and dismissed."[43] There was a good reason for the presence of the tunes, "Landaff" and "St. George's," in addition to "Funeral Thought," in fifer Gibb's music book. They no doubt had their place in his military society.

Soldiers sometimes attended Sabbath worship in a nearby church. Chaplain Robbins wrote his parents from Fort George on April 9, 1776:

> . . . I preach. I ag[n]. y[e] next Sab in y[e] same Ch[h]. in Albany a crowded attentive Audience N[os]. of Jersey & Pennsylvania Officers & Troops as well as ours—& many Albany people—a little before sunset went up to y[e] Barracks to visit some sick sold[rs].—& felt grieved exceedingly to see y[e] practice of y[e] people of y[e] poor vile City—who by 1000 were at Play & g[t]est Deversions swaring drunk & in short tis their high holiday far exceeding our Election Days near Hartford—At Sunset our Reg[ts]. drew up for Prayers & as we sung they collected round in vast no[s].—when G. enabled me to cry largely for them as well as y[e] Sold[rs].—They stared at me as at a strange Creature poor Wretches likely many hadn't heard a prayer in 12 months before. I returned to my lodgings excessively tired—but Col Buel nursed me like a fath[r].—. . .[44]

Civilians and military personnel were involved in public events such as one that Simeon Lyman and drummer Calvin Pease recorded in their journals. Both were en route to Boston with their militia units in August, 1775, and spent August 17 in the New London square. Pease reports:

> The forenoon we walked [into] the town and in the afternoon we was cald to arms and was marched up to the meting house and there was about 200 Weight of tee brought and put in the middle of the rode and there was tar barrels and Shavins and wood put on and then fire was put to it and consum[d] there was about 900 Soldiers under arms marched round y[e] Squire and there was a vast number of people and Spectators around. Some on housen and Some on the walk of the meting house with a french horn and drums and fifs they marched around the fire . . .[45]

Simeon Lyman's account tallies exactly, except for his estimate of 400 soldiers present. John Trumbull caught the spirit of such patriotic festivities in his satire of the Tory Squire, M'Fingal, who suffered the indignity of being tarred and feathered.

All Rome attends him thro' the street,
in triumph to his country-seat;
With like devotional the choir
Paraded round our feather'd Squire;
In front the martial music comes
Of horns and fiddles, fifes and drums,
With jingling sound of carriage bells,
And treble creak of rusted wheels. . . .[46]

Not until three years after the Lexington alarm did standardization of army discipline become a reality. Under the direction of Baron von Steuben, new drill techniques and regulations were instituted. During the winter at Valley Forge, 1777-78, the American army was in a state of confusion, compounded by shortages of equipment and men and the lack of systematized organization. Baron von Steuben's arrival in February of 1778 began a process of revitalization which affected company musicians as well as bandsmen. At the same time that von Steuben was appointed Inspector General of the Continental Army, Lieutenant John Hiwell, fife major of Crane's 3rd Artillery Band, was appointed Inspector and Superintendent of Music in the Army. Camus notes that although Hiwell's orders did not specify his duties, "it may be assumed that they were to standardize and improve the army's music."[47] Much of Hiwell's time was spent securing supplies, instruments and music.[48]

Demand for trained musicians persisted throughout the war, for both fifers and drummers for the companies of foot and trumpeters for the more mobile troops of horse and light infantry units. Connecticut must have had some musical reputation, for Major Henry Lee, from the Light Infantry Camp near White Plains, New York, advertised in the *Connecticut Courant* (1778):

WANTED IMMEDIATELY,

ONE or two more MUSICIANS, acquainted with the duties necessary to a corps of Light Dragoons. Any person or persons qualified for the above business, and willing to engage in the Cavalry, will meet with very generous terms by applying to the subscriber.[49]

In Wethersfield during the early part of 1777, Colonel Samuel B. Webb was engaged in recruiting musicians for a band of music in his Additional Regiment. Webb's officers, as was customary, purchased the instruments and the music. Both were available in Hartford through the firm of Fagan and Ballentine, whose *Courant* advertisement enumerated the musical supplies and materials they sold and the instruction they provided.

By Permission of the Committee of Hartford, will be taught

BY FAGAN and BALENTINE, . . .

MUSICK.

The following Instruments, viz. Violin, German Flute, French Horn, Hautbey, Clarinet, Bassoon, Psalter, Vaux Humane, Pipe and Tabor, Mandaline, and Fife. Musick also will be found for the different Instruments.

Gentlemen or Ladies may like wise be taught the Rules of Composition in Music, and may also have Music wrote or set for the Organ, Harpsichord, Spinet or Guitar.

N.B. Gentlemen may be attended at their own appartments; and a Night School will also be kept from six til nine o'Clock.

The above Instructors are to be found at Mr. Knox's, near the Ferry in Hartford.   February 3, 1777.[50]

Webb's accounts confirm that he obtained instruments and music for the band through Fagan and Ballentine. He paid a total sum of £58.11.0 "by cash" to Solomon Ballentine "for the Music."[51] This sum, according to specifications outlined by musician James Bremner in a letter to the Secretary of the Board of War, would have been enough for both music and instruments for the standard *Harmoniemusik* combination of two each of clarinets, oboes, French horns, and bassoons.[52] Bremner's letter suggested that the printed music would cost £4 or 5, and "if the Instruments are made in London where you may depend upon the goodness and neatness of the work the whole may amount between 50 & 60 £ Ster perhaps a little more the Music included—the Horns will be the dearest articles."[53]

General David Wooster may have intended to recruit a band of music in 1775 for his First Connecticut Regiment. The chaplain, the Reverend Benjamin Trumbull, recorded in his account book, "Gave by way of Subscription to purchase a French Horn for General Woosters Company 6/."[54] General Wooster, besides being regimental commanding officer, was Captain of the First Company. The enlistment roll for this company is missing, so it is not possible to ascertain if it contained the names of any known Connecticut musicians. Even if Wooster had been successful in enlisting a band, the names of his musicians would likely have been listed as privates. Camus had pointed out that "except in one instance, the men were not mustered separately as a band, nor often even as musicians, but as privates in individual companies."[55]

The eight musicians in Webb's band were carried as privates in Captain Charles Whiting's Company, the "Colonel's Company" of Webb's regiment. Their names are listed on a return for a special gratuity of clothing given to the band by General Sullivan.

A Return for a Suit of Clothing for the Band of Musick belonging to the Officers of Col. Sam B. Webbs Battalion

	Coats	Vests	Breechers	Shirts	Shoes	Stockings	Hatts	Rollers
Timothy Olmstead	1	1	1	2	1	2	1	2
Epraphras Jones	1	1	1	2	1	2	1	2
Solomon Goodrich	1	1	1	2	1	2	1	2
John Steel	1	1	1	2	1	2	1	2
Stephen Moulton	1	1	1	2	1	2	1	2
Prosper Hosmer	1	1	1	2	1	2	1	2
William Hooker	1	1	1	2	1	2	1	2
Jared Bunce	1	1	1	2	1	2	1	2
	8	8	8	16	8	16	8	16

It is desir'd that the Uniform may be Yellow if to be had: if not then White, but be it White or Yellow, wish it may be fac'd with Scarlet, Lin'd with white, & White Underdrefs—White Buttons— Warren 30th Dec'r 1778 E Huntington Maj'r Command'r

Col' Sam B. Webbs Battalion[56]

Major Ebenezer Huntington was in charge of the band, because Colonel Webb was taken prisoner in a raid on Long Island on December 10, 1777, and was on parole as a prisoner until 1780. Since the band belonged to the officers, its service was not interrupted by Webb's capture and absence from his regiment.

In the winter of 1779, Huntington sent a letter to General Sullivan to straighten out a misunderstanding over conflicting orders. Because the band was involved, Huntington's letter contains a summary of its status and conditions of service.

Your Excellency Observes that we mistake our Priviledges as to our Musick, and that all Bands drawing pay from the Publick, & eating the Publick Bread, are Subject to the Orders of the Commander in Chief, & altho' the Instruments are the Property of the officers, twould be very Impolite to decline sending them with their Instruments, as they are Subject to be draughted, & do privates duty, should you direct it—I observe the Band of Musick, draw Soldiers pay & Provision (& have ever been return[d] as Present fit for duty, which extra duty has been done by the Reg[t] & not allow[d] in the Details for the Reg[t]) besides which they receive an Additional pay from the Officers, who have already been at a very great Expence for a Master to teach them, & with this Expectation, that they alone would have a right to Command them *as Musick,* altho' Subject as Soldiers to the Command of every their Superiors, nor Could it be Esteem[d] Impolite to decline sending them with their Instruments, as the Matter might be Circumstanced, but which could be determined only, on the Reception of such an Order—[57]

The band played for ceremonial functions and for entertainment of the officers. Entries in Webb's journal provide the best picture of the officers' social life and the band's part in it.

Hurly Fryday 24th October 1777

His Excellency the Gen[l] gone over the River, orders for us to be in readiness to march on the shortest notice spent the day rideing, the Evening the two Miss Ten Eycks & Miss Betsy Elemendorph—with several Gentlemen were at my quarters—pass'd it sociable with the Band of Music &c.—&c.

Quarters between Maroneck & White Plains
Saturday Nov[r] 15th
. . . the Evening spent with decent sociability in Company with my Officers—& the Band of Musick

Monday Nov[r] 17th 1777

Returned this forenoon to Rye—took Quarters at Doughty's—the Evening a number of Ladies alias Women to hear the Band.—

Rye. Thursday November 20th 1777.

This being Thanksgiveing thro: the N England States, in Comp[y] with Brigadier Parsons—Maj[r] Huntington and Capt Bull of the Lt. Dragoons. I rode to Knapp's in Horseneck, where we found a large circle of Gentlemen and Ladies,—and an elegant, rather say good, entertainment prepared, we pass'd a sociable afternoon and spent the night 'till past 12 in dancing.

Norwalk Thursday Dec[r] 4th 1777

A day of leisure an elegant Dinner provided at Doct[r] Hills about Twenty Officers present—the Band of Music &c &c—the Wind has been too high for us to cross the Sound. . . . [written six days before Webb's capture.][58]

The three-year enlistments of the band's musicians expired early in 1780. At that time, Jones, Goodrich, Steel, Moulton, and Olmstead were discharged. Pressure had come from headquarters in a letter to the brigade commander from General Washington, who wrote, "How happens it that there are musicians returned as rank and file in Colonel Webb's Regiment who do no duty in the line? This seems to be an abuse and to require a remedy."[59] Webb was still on parole as a prisoner, and Huntington, now a Lieutenant Colonel, wrote to him from Morristown on February 16, with a "P S—Money nor promises will reinlist the band."[60] Webb worked out some arrangement with his musicians, for in a letter to Webb from Morristown in March, Huntington wrote, "I will be ready to wait on you to General Greene. When you call the Band will attend agreeable to your desire."[61] Records show that the other three of the original eight bandsmen—Hosmer, Hooker, and Bunce—had signed on as sergeants in May.[62]

Timothy Olmstead may have served in the band another year as well; a reference in the Olmstead geneology suggests he served with the Ninth Regiment in 1780. Webb's Regiment was reorganized in 1780 as the Ninth Regiment of the Connecticut Line, and went into winter quarters for 1780-81 at the camp "Connecticut Village" above the Robinson House.[63] Olmstead was appointed assistant chorister in East Hartford First Society on October 10, 1782, and unless this was a relative from the large Olmstead family, Timothy Olmstead may well have directed Webb's band as a civilian until after February 1782.[64] It is entirely possible that Goodrich, Jones, Steel, and Moulton also served in the band as civilians.

A letter from Huntington to Webb from the Connecticut Village on February 15, 1782, contains the request, "Must beg you will send Sergt. Hosmer to Camp immediately, as his presence is absolutely necessary, as Capt. Hopkins will be able to inform you, to whom I refer you for the more particular situation of the Regiment than my knowledge will afford."[65] Sergeant Hosmer was reduced on February 8, 1782.[66] Perhaps the band was still together. Huntington's urgent request undoubtedly reflected a need for Hosmer's musical services, either with the band or the field music.

Professional and amateur musicians returned from the war with a wealth of experiences behind them. It is highly unlikely that many, especially the professionals, were unaffected by an exchange of musical ideas, repertory, and practical information. Connecticut fife majors Aaron Thompson (Woodbury) and Benjamin Swetland (Somers) served with New Jersey and Massachusetts units respectively. The Manning brothers from Norwich, Roger and Diah, drummers, transferred to Washington's Life Guards at Valley Forge. With the Guards as fifers were Jacob Goodrich (Wethersfield) and Frederick Parks (Groton).[67] Roger Manning came home in 1780 and advertised as a teacher.

ROGER MANNING

PROPOSES (provided suitable encouragement offers) to instruct young gentlemen in every rule appertaining to the DRUM.—He flatters himself that such as have a genius suited to music, will, in a very short time, be instructed to beat almost any tune or march, with exactness and propriety, that is now in vogue in the Continental Army. —He has acted as Drum-Major, for several years, in the service of the United States; and can produce (if required) sufficient *credentials* of his skill in the above branch.—For terms, enquire at his lodgings, near the Meeting-House.

N.B. *None need apply, but such as can furnish themselves with Drums.*

Norwich, March 14, 1780.[68]

Teachers of vocal music continued their work throughout the war in the usual manner, despite periodic military intrusions. As the major war action shifted to the south, Connecticut was nevertheless regularly traversed by soldiers and civilians bent on the innumerable errands of a war-time economy. Itinerant singing masters were supplied with some of their materials through local merchants. Nathaniel Patten, for example, bookbinder and stationer, moved from Boston to Hartford in the summer of 1776 and opened a shop "under the Printing Office." He advertised:

> will bind, gild, and letter books in as splendid a manner as if done in London. Old books he can metamorphose into new, at least the difference will not be perceptable to those who do not open them. He has for sale the following BOOKS, viz. Bibles, Spelling Books, Psalters, Primers, Watts' Psalms and Hymns, bound in one volume, or separate, Brady & Tate's Psalms, Rev. Samson Occum's Collection of Hymns, . . . Singing Books, the Gamut, or Scale of Musick, Blank Books to prick Tunes in, Copy Books, . . . Song books, . . . Great Allowance to those who buy to sell again.[69]

The war may have delayed Connecticut's music-publishing business, but it made its debut in 1778, nonetheless, with an abridged edition of Andrew Law's *Select Harmony*. An advertisement on the front page explained that

> THE times being such, that it is impossible to get plates cut for all the musick at first proposed, there will be an addition made as soon as they can be done; and what is now printed with types, with a further illustration of some things, will then be printed on paper of the same size and quality of that on which the musick is now printed.[70]

The subscription proposal for the 1779 edition of 100 pages appeared in the New London *Connecticut Gazette* in July of 1778;

> Now collecting . . . A Collection of Psalm-Tunes and Anthems, from the most celebrated authors in Great Britain and America, with a compleat System of rules drawn up in the most concise, plain and easy manner, for the benefit of learners.
> The book will contain about 200 pages, neatly engraved on plate. The fluctuating state of our public affairs renders it impossible to ascertain the price of the book, but the collector assures the public it will be the cheapest ever published in America . . . .
> Subscriptions are taken in by Messrs. Eliphalet Lyman at Lebanon, Mark Anthony Deaolph, at Chealsea in Norwich; Caleb Huntington, at Norwich; Amasa Deaolph at Pomfret; Thomas Jones at Killingly.[71]

Mr. Lyman may have been the singing master hired at Litchfield in 1774. Mr. Huntington, born February 4, 1748/9, to a prominent Norwich family, was later a deacon in the First Society. Mark Anthony and Amasa Deaolph, along with their brother Charles, were singing masters active in central and eastern Connecticut. Charles and one of his brothers took Oliver King's subscription in 1775. Sons of Simon De Wolf of Middletown, Charles was born April 19, 1747; Amasa on December 26, 1748; and Mark Anthony on March 9, 1752.[72] Any one of the brothers could have written the pieces attributed to Deaolph in *Select Harmony*. One of these, Psalm 136, was a very popular double fuging tune.[73] Its first fuging section is arranged with successive vocal entries building upward from the bass, and the second reverses the order. Music of Connecticut composers Amos Bull, Alexander Gillet, Oliver Brownson, and Oliver King was also included. Gillet (1749-1826) was a Torrington pastor who combined the careers of clergyman and composer. He and Law were associates and friends from the time of Law's return to Connecticut from Providence, and beginning with four in *Select Harmony,* Law printed many of Gillet's pieces.[74] Amos Bull is also represented by four pieces, one of which is the popular "Middletown," a plain tune setting with a brief antiphonal section. A plain tune, by definition, is a setting of a psalm or hymn text without text repetitions, but usually without structural elaboration.

MIDDLETOWN (Bull)

Law's collection, comprising a selection of psalm and hymn tunes in plain tune settings, tunes with extension, and anthems, was a major achievement and the first of a whole series of works he contributed to the psalmody repertory.[75] The American compositions that he included in *Select Harmony* give a clue to the vitality of the singing schools and their teachers, since most of the composers represented were engaged in that business. After the war, publishing music books for the trade became big business, and Andrew Law was busy managing a number of singing school teachers who went out from the state, armed with tunebooks published in Cheshire.

Andrew Law registered another major achievement when the General Assembly granted approval of his petition of October 15, 1781, for a patent for tunes in his publications. Irving Lowens noted that "as one of the first citizens of the five-year-old United States to be granted a legal copyright, Andrew Law, a rising star in the American musical firmament, added an interesting footnote to our social history."[76] Law published another collection in 1781, the *Select Number of Plain Tunes,* designed to be sung with the texts of the metrical psalter.

By January 1780, President Ezra Stiles of Yale College (installed July 8, 1778) could report that "they sing Watts's Version of the Psalms in the three Meetings in Town; as well as at the College. At Mr. Hubbard's Episc⁰ Ch^h they sing Tate & Brady's Version of the Psalms. Twenty years ago they sang the old New England Version at the Meetings."[77] Bela Hubbard was one of the few Church of England clergymen able to continue his ministry in the heated Tory-versus-Patriot atmosphere. Most Episcopal churches were closed. In some "established" churches, the "choir movement" made headway, while the absence of men from others curtailed extended musical performance. A 1778 muster roll of Captain John Hill's company from Winchester, for example, lists five musicians; three, Belah Hill and Levi Brownson, fifers, and Andrew Everit, drummer, were choristers in Winchester's First Society. In addition, the company's officers, Captain Hill, Lieutenant Benjamin Benedict, and Ensign Ozias Brownson, were choristers in the Society.[78] A complete list of church musicians, both amateur and professional, who served in the war from all parts of the state would cover many pages.

The issue of whether to allow musical instruments in worship became more heated in these years. East Windsor considered the weighty question of whether to admit the use of the pitch-pipe in setting the psalm in 1780, and "Voted in the negative."[79] Brownson's chorister on the *Select Harmony* title page, it may be noticed, is sounding his pitchpipe for the singers. In North Haven, the Reverend Benjamin Trumbull led his church through a painful personal and communal crisis. Histories record disagreements over administration of the Sacrament, but they ignore a timely musical issue that was part and parcel of the affair. A church meeting on January 4, 1781, voted that "for the Peace of the Brethren . . . Some of the Old Tunes should be learned and sung in the Assembly with Reading one-half of the Time."[80] They voted to sing the "New Tunes" the other half of the time without reading. The Committee that was chosen to select the music was also requested to "desire that the School would learn and Sing y^m by rule."

Trumbull copied out the committee report "verbatim and the votes of the Ch^h Concerning Singing, and the next Day Sent y^m to the School."

To The Singing School in N. H. Gentlemen Jan^{ry} 9th 1781.

At a meeting of the Committee of the Church appointed to advise and determine, what Tunes are proper and advisable to be sung among us, it was agreed. After hearing the School sing over those Tunes w^cy^y had learned, that It maybe well for them to sing the following Tunes, provided that a number of other Tunes more grave & of slower movements, should be learned and sung with y^m, Viz. The 122 Psalm Tune, the 34th. Do the 115 Do 46 Do Landaff, Rochester, Colchester, Little Marlbury, St Thomas's, Aylesbury, Brookfield, Amherst, and Newbury and Balldock.

But as these Tunes are generally of a very Quick movement, it is our opinion That it is best and will be most for the Peace of the Society for them to learn three or four more of ye old Tunes, with four or five others of grave and Slow movements Particularly, RickmansWorth, Plymouth, Wantage, St. Martins' & The funeral Thought. As to the old Tunes we leave the School to their own choice as to what three or four of them they will sing. We think also that it would be well for the School to Learn one more short metre tune on a Sharp Key of a Slower movement, than any y^y have sung excepting Little Marlborough.

We send you with this a very unanimous vote of the Ch^h Concerning this matter, and entreat you, Gentlemen, to give it proper Weight; and we earnestly desire that you would comply with our advice, And learn the Tunes Suggested. We urge it as a matter w^c we really think will promote the Peace of this Society and the glory of God. We are, Gentlemen Your Friends and humble Servants.

Benjamin Trumbull, Ithamar Todd, Jesse Todd, Ebenezer Todd, Solomon Tuttle[81]

Trumbull's clear leadership is evident in the committee report; a music manuscript he wrote at about this time contains twelve of the nineteen new tunes named. In addition, he wrote out several pages of musical theory on concords and discords, rules of composition, and the nature of sound. The last page of the manuscript contains "A Dissertation on the physical and mathematical Grounds of Musick."[82]

Trumbull was not without justification when he stated, "I have always been a great Friend to Ch^h musick and am still so. I have done more to promote y^t part of public Worship during the twenty years of my ministry, I have no doubt, yⁿ any five or ten men in the Society ...."[83] His petition of grievances to the church in July also complained that he had used all his abilities to introduce the revival of singing in a "prudent, inoffensive manner," but "my Opinion has been disregarded, my advice and Generosity trampled upon, and my name loaded with infamy and reproach in town and out." Another complicating factor in the affair was an altercation involving Mrs. Trumbull. As her husband put it, "a matter of grief to me was the Treatment of Mr[s]. Trumbull in her weak and uncomfortable State . . . by the Time she had been at meeting only two or three Sabbaths, the Singers Left their Seats, and the Clamour was handed round that I was trying to break up the Singing."[84] Whatever may have been the unacceptable manner of Mrs. Trumbull's participation in the singing, the Society and their pastor eventually came to a face-saving compromise. In October, even though other grievances remained to be settled, Trumbull acknowledged "that Since the Church Meeting August 16th the Church and Singers had Conducted the Affair of singing as it respected M[rs]. Trumbull in a manner . . . that . . . he and his Family were obliged."[85]

Trumbull, for his part, had publicly acknowledged, in the July communication to the church, that he "was blameable, particularly in reproving the young people one evening with too much Warmth." His zeal for music education must have caused him to forget that singing school was also a social institution, a place where young people could meet in mixed company with the approval of their parents. As one of Yale Tutor Simeon Baldwin's friends wrote in a letter, "I am almost sick of the World & were it not for the Hopes of going to singing-meeting to night & indulging myself a little in some of the carnal Delights of the Flesh, such as kissing, squeezing &c. &c. I should willingly leave it now, before 10 o'clock & exchange it for a better."[86]

Other "mixed company" events, directly attributed to war-time conditions, enlivened society in various corners of Connecticut. As Simeon Baldwin's sister Mary wrote him at Yale:

I think you have doubtless heard that there is a number of the french troops stationed at Lebanon they seem to be the cheif topick of discourse I think now in town & I hear since I come home that the Duke is going to have a grand Ball next friday at Lathrops so as to get acquainted with our Norwich Ladys I suppose he has had one at Windham What will be the event of these things I cant say but he Who governs all things will no doubt order all things for the best.[87]

Abbé Robin, chaplain with the French army, observed that

the Americans, whom curiosity brings by thousands to our camp, are constantly received with good humour and festivity; and our military music, of which they are extravagantly fond, is then played for their diversion. At such times officers, soldiers, Americans, of both sexes, all intermingle and dance together;—it is the feast of equality; and these are the first fruits of the alliance which is, we hope, to subsist perpetually between the two nations.[88]

The range of subject matter in the topical songs of the war years followed the procession of rapid political and military changes, and included the usual political satire and anthems and odes commemorating great events. The Reverend John Devotion appended to his Election Sermon (1777) a new anthem, "Independence."[89] Connecticut poets were responsible for some famous song-texts, and in the case of "Bunker Hill," for both words and music. The parody on "The Banks of the Dee," was circulated in the same way as many song-texts—from person to person. Benjamin Tallmadge wrote from Crampond to Samuel B. Webb at Wethersfield on July 6, 1780, and included the "P.S.—. . . the enclosed parody or answer to the song called the banks of the Dee, please to present to Miss Chester [John Chester's sister] as she may probably take the trouble to learn it."[90] A text attributed to Oliver Arnold of Norwich goes as follows:

'Twas winter, and blue Tory noses were freezing,
As they marked o'er the land where they ought not to be.
The valiants complained at the fifers' cursed wheezing,
And wished they'd remained on the banks of the Dee.
Lead on thou paid captain! tramp on thou proud minions!
Thy ranks, basest men, shall be strung like ripe onions,
For here thou hast found heads with warlike opinions
On the shoulders of nobles who ne'er saw the Dee.[91]

A long ballad, "The American Taxation," is thought to have been written by Peter or Samuel St. John of New Canaan.[92] The British Government is taken to task in thirty-seven verses for its restrictive legislation, and the American cause is lauded for its strength, wisdom, and its great men. Verse 27, for example, which calls Washington "the second Alexander," reinforces Kate Keller's choice of "The British Grenadiers" as the intended tune. The reader may "try out" verses 1 and 23 to the tune on page 68.

Verse 1	Verse 23
While I relate my story,	We have Green, Gates and Putnam,
Americans give ear;	To manage in the field,
Of Britain's fading glory	A Gallant train of footmen,
You presently shall hear.	Who had rather die than yield;
I'll give a true relation-	A stately troop of horses,
Attend to what I say,	Train'd in a martial way,
Concerning the taxation	For to augment our forces
Of North-America.	In North-America.[93]

The most famous tune of the war was "Yankee Doodle." It appears, beginning with the second half, and the cryptic title, "Thehos Gendar," in Gibbs' fife manuscript, but the origins of both music and text are still a mystery.[94] When the British army landed in Boston in September, 1768, they were reported to have played "Yankee Doodle."[95] Texts were written to the tune by both sides during the war; a common denominator of caricature pervades many of them. John Trumbull's Squire M'Fingal claimed the tune for New England.

When Yankies, skill'd in martial rule,
First put the British troops to school;
Instructed them in warlike trade,
And new maneuvres of parade;
The true war-dance of Yanky-reels,
And *manual exercise* of heels

. . .

So tho' our war few triumphs brings,
We gain'd great fame in other things.
Did not our troops show much discerning,
And skill your various arts in learning?
Outwent they not each native Noodle
By far in playing Yanky-doodle;
Which, as 'twas your New England tune,
'Twas marvelous they took so soon?
And ere the year was fully thro',
Did not they learn to foot it to;[96]

One of the texts associated with the tune was a satiric tale about a boy and his Father on a visit "down to camp."[97] The refrain was;

Yankee doodle keep it up,
Yankee doodle dandy,
Mind the music and the step
And with the girls be handy. . . .

At some point, possibly as late as the twentieth century, a nineteenth century nursery rhyme was substituted for the verse in this long popular folk song.[98]

Yankee Doodle came to town,
Upon a Kentish poney,
He stuck a feather in his hat,
And called him Macaroni.

With slight legislative modification, this is now Connecticut's State song.[99]

Yankee Doodle went to town,   Yankee doodle keep it up,
Riding on a pony,   Yankee doodle dandy,
Stuck a feather in his hat,   Mind the music and the step,
And called it macaroni,   And with the folks be handy.

"Yankee Doodle" served a number of texts written in response to the Yorktown victory of October, 1781. In one that appeared in the *Connecticut Courant,* dance metaphors, so common in topical song-texts, create an interesting parallel, as Kate Keller points out, between the stylized military maneuvers of eighteenth-century warfare and the ever-popular country dance.

THE DANCE

A Ballad, to the tune of "Yankey Doodle."

I.

CORNWALLIS led a country dance,
The like was never seen, sir,
Much retrograde, and much advance,
And all with General Greene, sir.

III

Greene, in the south, then danc'd a set,
And got a mighty name, sir.
Cornwallis jigg'd with young Fayette,
But suffered in his fame, sir.

XII

His music soon forgets to play—
His feet can move no more, sir,
And all his bands now curse the day,
They jigg'd it to our shore, sir

XIII

Now Tories all what can ye say?
Come—is not this a griper?
That while your hopes are danc'd away,
'Tis you must pay the piper.

FINIS.[100]

The victory at Yorktown inspired a legend, that at the surrender the British bands played a tune called "The World Turned Upside Down." This tune has never been positively identified, but a number of candidates have been put forward.[101] A tune named "The Wourld Turnd Upside Down" has recently turned up in Fife Major Nathaniel Brown's music book.[102]

After Yorktown, Washington was accorded full honors as the supreme national hero. "Hail, the glorious Washington" sang the chorus in the final scene of Francis Hopkinson's oratorical entertainment, *Minerva,* which premiered in Philadelphia on December 11, 1781.[103] Gradually, preoccupation with war gave way to the peace-time tasks of nation building.

IV

Music in the Eighties

Peace to Constitution

The idea had become prevalent, among the naturalists and literati in Europe who have written on American subjects, that almost every species of animal and vegetable life, has degenerated by being transported across the Atlantic to this country. . . . The time has come to expose the European creed, that we are infantine in our acquisition and savage in our manners; because we are inhabitants of a New World, lately occupied by a race of savages.

It cannot, I presume, be ungrateful or unprofitable for our countrymen to take a review of the illustrious personages, who have signalized themselves, during the revolution, in the several departments of policy, legislation and war . . . .

The more immediate object of this essay was to remind my countrymen of their capacity for great undertakings, and of the rapid, though to careless observers imperceptible progress, that is made in cultivating the *fine arts*. Genius is the growth of every country. There is no doubt but America may boast an equal proportion with the old world . . . .

From "An Essay on American Genius," in *The New-Haven Gazette, and the Connecticut Magazine.*[1]

NATIONALISM ran through most pronouncements on America's artistic capabilities and achievements. As the writer on America's genius, probably Meigs or Dana, pointed out, "the age of ultimate refinement" in America "had not yet come," but the increase in wealth and "progress in population" would undoubtedly lead to the development of "music, architecture, gardening, sculpture, and other elegant arts." The writer considered it fortuitous when "these amusements contribute rather to enoble than degrade the human mind," and he recommended directing "the taste of a nation to substitute, instead of the vulgar enjoyments of cock-fighting, gambling, and tavern-haunting, pleasures of a more refined and innocent nature."

The development of a national taste in the arts was not incompatible with the aspirations of a new republic. Jean Calvin's precept about music's effect on the human emotions was obviously still appropriate to its proper use in the new society. Music's potential role in the production of new generations of socially-sensitive and morally-upstanding citizens became a cornerstone of musical aesthetics. It stimulated, in part, the introduction of music programs in nineteenth-century American public schools, and was a factor, as well, in the singing movement in the factories of the mother country. As the writer of an article, "On Music," thought to be Noah Webster himself, observed,

> The establishment of schools for teaching Psalmody . . . is a pleasing
> institution, but people seem not to understand the design, or rather
> are not aware of the advantages which may result from it, if properly
> conducted and encouraged. Most people consider music merely as a
> source of pleasure—not attending to its influence on the human mind
> and its consequent effects on society. But it should be regarded as an
> article of education, *useful* as well as ornamental.[2]

Clearly, what began as an instrument of church music reform early in
the eighteenth century, the singing school, had become, by the penulti-
mate decade, an institution which produced musical literacy across a
large and representative cross-section of the population. The time had
come for society's leaders to reaffirm music's didactic function, and so to
justify expenditure of time and economic resources on artistic endeavors.
The issue of edification versus entertainment was destined to retain a
permanent place in America's musical discourse.

The diversity of musical culture in the 1780s is easily discernible
in the number and nature of public and private occasions in which musical performance was a vital element: in the musical education offered in
singing schools, academies, and at Yale College; in the variety of
musical merchandise available from Connecticut merchants and publishers; in the growth of the sister arts of theater and literature; in the
national prominence of Connecticut composers and tunebook com-
pliers; and in new societies and organizations. The Connecticut Society
of Arts and Sciences, instituted in May, 1786, listed the most prominent
citizens of the State on its membership rolls, as well as honorary members "His Excellency Gen. Washington, Marquis de la Fayette, Col.
Tim⁰ Pickering, and Hon. Theodore Sedgwick."[3]

Connecticut musicians scored an impressive number of "firsts"
symptomatic of the heightened artistic activity of the eighties. New
Haven engraver and clock-maker Simeon Jocelin (1746-1823) was the
first tunebook compiler to publish a collection, *The Chorister's Companion* (1782), in which pieces were individually identified by the
designation "American author," although Andrew Law of Cheshire
had been the first to print pieces by Connecticut composers (1778) and
the first to obtain a copyright for musical composition in the new
republic (1781). Daniel Read of New Haven, with engraver and
printer Amos Doolittle, published the first musical periodical in
America, *The American Musical Magazine* (1786). Read was also
the first Connecticut composer to publish a collection of music composed solely by himself, *The American Singing Book* (1785). In this
accomplishment, Read was second only to William Billings of Boston.
The Select Songster (1786), "Compiled by Philo. Musico." (Chauncey
Langdon), was the first American collection of songs "With Music
prefixed to each." The music in these publications, and others of the

eighties, reflects a wide range of styles and employment.

In terms of quantity, content, technical production, and influence, music books engraved in Connecticut must be part of the reason William Bentley, pastor of East Church, Salem, Massachusetts, could write, in 1797, that "vocal music had its progress in Connecticut."[4] Andrew Law alone (that is, with brother William, in Cheshire) produced an impressive list of music books: *A Collection of Hymn Tunes,* companion to *A Collection of Hymns,* for social worship (1783); *The Rudiments of Music* for singing schools (first two editions 1783, 1785); *A Select Number of Plain Tunes* ([1781]); and a revised edition of the popular *Select Harmony* (1782). The *Norwich Packet* proudly advertised "Mr. Law's Collection of Music" as "now preferred by most of the schools in the New-England States."[5]

Connecticut's singing masters may have pioneered in pedagogical methods. Some teachers, for example Timothy Swan and Daniel Read, had reputations as fine singers as well. Discussions of vocal technique were part of the introductory material in tunebooks by Law, Jocelin, Brownson, Read, and Langdon, and Law's suggestion that the voice be clear as possible and aim at "ease and freedom" was a popular one. Jocelin and Doolittle echoed it in a short essay in *The Chorister's Companion* (1782) on "tuning and forming" the voice, and a longer one entitled "Observations on Singing."

> Let the voice be clear and smooth as possible, neither forcing the sound through the nose, nor blowing through the teeth with the mouth shut;—a trembling in the voice is also carefully to be avoided.— All high notes should be sounded soft, but not faint;—the low notes full, but not harsh;—and let all be done with ease and freedom, endeavouring to cultivate a musical voice; observing for imitation, the sweet sound of the violin, the soft melody of the flute, and the tuneful notes of the nightingale.[6]

The Chorister's Companion, a small, oblong tunebook for choirs, was intended for a wide commercial market, with subscriptions taken at "Houses of Entertainment in Killingworth, Guilford, Branford, Derby, Newtown, New-Milford, Danbury, Woodbury, and Washington," and at the Printing Office in New Haven.[7] Music teachers and students could also purchase the introductory "Rules, in one sheet, . . . at One Shilling."[8] The system of rules for Law's *Select Harmony,* bound with four sheets of the music, was available at Cheshire and at Goodrich's Store in New Haven for three shillings, and two shillings and six pence by the dozen.[9] Purchasers who already owned the 1778/9 edition could have the new music, "Denmark and others by Dr. Madan," separately.[10] Sales no doubt profited from the issue of parts and sections of tunebooks, but they created a host of bibliographical problems for present-day scholars.

The Chorister's Companion was meant to furnish a collection of mostly psalm and hymn tunes "that should be neither too dull on the one side, nor too licentious on the other." Jocelin and Doolittle commented:

> It is very obvious, that Psalmody hath undergone a considerable revolution, in most of our religious assemblies, within the course of a few years, not only with respect to the method and order of singing, but even the tunes formerly in common use, are now generally laid aside, instead of which, those of a more lively and airy turn are substituted. And, altho' many improvements have been made in Church Music, yet there appears a danger of erring, by introducing, in public worship, light and trifling airs, more becoming the theatre or shepherd's pipe; a liberty (as we apprehend) by no means admissible in the solemnities of Divine Service.[11]

This admonition should not be construed to mean that only plain tunes with uniform note values were acceptable, as Oliver Brownson's popular "Virginia" shows.[12]

The "solemnities of Divine Service" were observed in Connecticut churches according to local needs and resources, as they always had been. The war had caused disruptions in many communities, however, and annual meetings frequently voted, as in Newington Society, to "do something towards the reviving of singing amongst us" by hiring a singing master.[13] In West Woodstock, the New Roxbury Society concurred with the church in voting that "as there are but few psalm-books amongst us, the singing be carried on by reading the portion line by line till the last singing in the afternoon, and then a whole verse to be read at a time."[14] A choir of six men presumably led the singing. Three years later, in 1785, a meeting was called by request to "agree as to the mode of singing, whereby they may all rest easy," and a vote was taken

That yᵉ mode of singing for the future, that the deacon read the portion line by line in the forenoon; and in the afternoon to read a verse at a time; except the Double verse Tunes; and them to be sung through without reading; and that to be the standing rule till ordered otherwise by the committee.[15]

Solemnity and dignity in worship were abstractions that seemed to depend as much on fashion as on liturgical precept, and suitable musical performance was subject to similar influences. The Wethersfield First Society was visited in 1784 by a distinguished guest from Spain, Count Francisco di Miranda, and his account of a typical Sunday with the leading families follows:

It was Sunday, the Sabbath, so at 10 O'clock in the morning I went, in the company of Colonel and Mrs. Chester, to the functional and rather unattractive meeting house. The service lasted until noon. As it was a day of the Sacrament I went to have dinner with Mr. Joseph Webb. At 3 O'clock we returned to the church. Since this was the assembly with the greatest attendance and the most splendor, the young ladies were better coifed and dressed at this time, and all of them were present. (This was the only place where they could present themselves publicly and be seen) So indeed the attendance was more numerous than in the morning. They sang very well their psalms and antiphons. The teaching method employed was the following: the music master (maestro) instructed all of the young ladies and the young men as well, in their homes. Afterward each one brought his or her music book to the church where they formed three choruses in the upper gallery. Their music teacher here became the Maestro or director of the chapel. They sang in a very good musical tone although without an organ or any other instrumental accompaniment. The musical composition as well as the singing was the most solemn and ecclesiastical that I had heard on this continent. The program ended at half past four and we went to take tea at the house of Mr. Webb whose wife and family were exceedingly pleasant and hospitable. Afterwards we went up to the steeple, or tower of the church which is quite outstanding, and from which could be seen a beautiful view of all of the surrounding area, including the Connecticut River. That night we returned once more to the church to enjoy the music of the monthly rehearsal of the music director and the singers as they reviewed together all of the psalms and songs that they had studied up to that point. This lasted somewhat more than an hour after which I returned home weary and satiated up to the eyes with church.[16]

Count Miranda has described in words the setting the artist portrayed in the frontispiece of Oliver Brownson's *Select Harmony*. This important tunebook, which contained a large number of new pieces by Americans, including Brownson himself, thus preserves not only a representative selection of music, but also the only known inconographic representation of a worship service of the period.

Oliver Brownson followed Simeon Jocelin's lead and had the "Author's Names set over the tunes" in his collection. An advertisement printed following the preface notified purchasers that "The Author having made alterations in some of the Tunes that were given out of his hands, desires that those who have received former Copies, would conform to this Publication."[17] In keeping with contemporary practice, Brownson's pieces were distributed in manuscript copies, and he was requesting that the newly-printed version in *Select Harmony* be regarded as definitive.

Brownson's collection, according to a *Courant* advertisement, was "To be Sold by the Dozen or Single, At his house or at Benham's, in New-Hartford."[18] Eight pieces of Asahel Benham's (1754-1803) were printed by Brownson, but Benham's own *Federal Harmony* did not appear in print until 1790. Similarly, Timothy Swan's compositions were printed for the first time by Brownson in a third edition (c. 1785).[19] Benham was a teacher of singing schools in the New England and Mid-Atlantic States. Andrew Law mentioned his activities in Pennsylvania after 1789.[20] Benham was reputedly endowed with a prepossessing personal appearance, and was a highly-regarded professional musician.[21] His small, oblong, engraved tunebook, *Federal Harmony,* went through six editions, Benham's pieces in *Select Harmony* were Yarmouth, Brandford, Chatham, Wakefield, Death Alarm, Repentance, Babylon, and the "Anthem from Sundry Parts of Revelations." Two other anthems by known resident Connecticut composers were published in the eighties, and those were Daniel Read's "Down Steers the Bass," a setting of Mather Byles' famous poem "On Musick," and "O Praise the Lord, O My Soul," in *The American Singing Book*. Benham's anthem opens with solo sections for bass and tenor over two-part chorus, and continues with texture and meter changes, closing with a broad Alleluia and Amen."[22]

Timothy Swan (1758-1842), who spent the most productive years of his professional musical life in Suffield, Connecticut, is represented by seven pieces in *Select Harmony*: Poland (CM), Lisbon (SM), Rainbow (CM fuging tune), Bristol (LM), Balloon (LM), Majesty (PM fuging tune), and Flanders (LM).[23]

Swan's association with Brownson extended as well to sales, as the *Courant* indicated: "Brownson's Collection of Music, To be sold at this Office, and at BROWNSON'S and BENHAM'S New-Hartford, and at SWAN'S at Suffield."[24] Swan's daughter, Emily Cordelia Swan, described their meeting in her notes:

> Mr. Brunson a composer in music—he lived 20 miles from S———d he called to see father—after conversation & singing—he said to father— "I will tell you what I tho't of you—I supposed you to be a man pretty well advanced with a wig on & a cocked hat. This was somewhere about 1785.[25]

Anthem from sundry Parts of Revelations, by Benham. 65

Holy holy holy Lord God al — — mighty which was and is — — and in — — to to come

Thou art wor — thy O Lord to receive Glory and honour and Pow'r for thou hast cre — a — — ted all things;

Thou art wor — thy O Lamb of God to take the Book and open the seals there of For thou wast sla —

Blessing and

Bless — ing blessing

and hast redeem — — ed us to God by thy Blood

Blessing and ho — — now and

Blessing and ho — —

Swan's reputation as a composer was obviously not only well-established, but also of considerable worth by the mid-eighties. Brownson specially mentioned in his advertising that "a number of new tunes have lately been added by the ingenious Mr. Swan."[26] According to a family friend, E. Webster, "none of his music at this time was published, but handed about in manuscript, and sung in private circles and by a select number, who met statedly with the author to learn and practice it."[27]

Swan apparently began composing soon after his early singing school training, and, subsequent to enlistment in the army in 1774, he moved with his mother to Northfield, Massachusetts, where he was apprenticed as a hatter to his brother-in-law. Swan came to Enfield about 1780, and then settled in Suffield. A letter appended to Webster's "Memoir," sent from "an aged friend" to Miss Swan, said:

> Your dear father came to Suffield about the year 1780 well do I remember his looks, manners and fine singing all of which charm'd my youthful heart, as well as that of your mothers.—It was not long before his songs were sung with much applause and, the Shepherd's complaint, gain'd great celebrity—after that, his "seasons"—"Solomon's Songs" &c &c were much admired—and he was frequently applied to —to write music for occasional services—[28]

Among the Swan Papers is a single sheet inscribed, "Presented to Mary Gay by Timothy Swan in 1783" (They were married in 1784). At the top of the page is a tune for treble instrument (violin), and four verses.

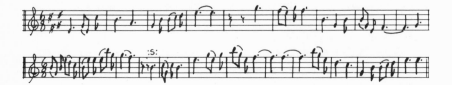

> O nightingale best poet of the Grove
> That plaintive strain can ne'er belong to Thee
> Blest in the full Possession of thy Love
> O Lend that strain sweet Nightingale to me[29]

Other pieces for treble instrument, probably violin, and bass are written in a manuscript collection Swan compiled early in his composing career. Beside sketches for two psalm tunes, there is a selection of popular British song and dance melodies, and a few pieces that are Swan's own arrangements or compositions.[30] He was not the only musician in late eighteenth-century New England who worked in a variety of genres and wrote music for different kinds of private and public occasions. Many tunebook composers and compilers who are associated by historians and analysts with Psalmody did not confine their musical interests or activities to church music. Furthermore, the music itself, particularly vocal music, cannot easily be categorized as religious or non-religious. Sometimes the text indicated where or when a specific anthem, ode, or plain four-part choral piece was to be performed. But, especially in the case of Isaac Watts' poetry, religious verse did not signify its limitation to church- or worship-related use. Many printed and manuscript music collections contained pieces in several musical forms.

A case in point is the "Welcome Song," a canon 4-in-1, printed in John Blow's *Amphion Anglicus* (London, 1700), and used by Oliver Brownson on the title page for his *Select Harmony*. It was probably not sung in church, unless the final singing school "exhibition" (alias concert), which it often opened, was held there.[81] Andrew Law included Benjamin West's "Ode on Spring," perhaps for a similar use, in his *Select Harmony* (1778/9). Staple items in manuscript commonplace books, from Miles and Whitman to Deacon Story and Benjamin Trumbull, were pieces such as "Pompey's Ghost," "Advice to the Fair Sex," "The Indian Philosopher," and hymns on the "Vanity of the World" and the "Divine Use of Musick." Read and Doolittle's fourth number of *The American Musical Magazine* contained vocal and instrumental music ascribed to Arne, Hook, and Fischer, among the other numbers devoted to anthems, psalm tunes, and set pieces. The traditions and conventions that determined the "sacred" or "secular" realms of artistic and cultural life, in a Connecticut in which the church was established by law until 1818, were by no means categorically applicable to musical expressions, or to individual musicians.

Daniel Read (1757-1836), who grew up in Rehoboth, Massachusetts, settled in New Haven at the end of the war and pursued an active career as a prominent musician and businessman.[82] Read, like Swan, was well-established by the mid-eighties, as a letter of recommendation shows.

New Haven Nov'r 27, 1786

To all to whom this shall be presented.

The following is for information to those who are Strangers to the bearer, Mr. Daniel Read. He is a respectable citizen of this city, a gentleman of respectable character & abilities, an uncommon proficient in the art of vocal music, and is the author of a singing book which has met with extensive approbation, entituled the *American Singing Book*. We sincerely wish him the attension of all respectable gentlemen among whom he may be conversant. As he is a man of integrity, fidelity and benevolence we cannot apprehend that any who favour him with their attention or assistance will be disappointed in acquaintance.

We recommend Mr. Read most chearfully to the Gentleman or Gentlemen to whom this shall be given, and should esteem any favours shewn as obliging us, We are &c.

Ezra Stiles, President of Yale Coll.
Samuel Wales, Professor of Divinity, Yale College
Samuel Austin, Pastor of Church in New Haven.[33]

Read's music appeared first in print in Jocelin's *Chorister's Companion*, but *The American Singing Book*, "Designed for the use of singing schools in America," was a collection of forty-nine pieces, all of Read's composition. Two of these were anthems and forty-seven were tunes, twenty of them fuges.[34] As Irving Lowens has stated, Read should be remembered not only for "his key role in the development of the unique melodic-harmonic idiom characteristic of American composed music in the decades after the Revolution," but especially for the role of his "music and compilations (even greater than those of his famed contemporary William Billings) in establishing the high popularity of the American fuging-tune."[35] A favorite, "Greenwich," was copied out by Simon or Thaddeus Larned, whose father, Simon, was deacon and clerk of the Thompson church from 1769 to 1789.[36]

Read's other major publishing venture of the eighties, with Amos Doolittle, was *The American Musical Magazine*, "A new Collection of Divine Music, together with a variety of favorite pieces for amusement and entertainment both vocal and instrumental."[37] The proposal, addressed "To all Lovers of Music," closed with a note from the publishers of the *Gazette* explaining their reason for the new quarto format.

"The Music abovementioned will be printed on a page of the same size as the NEW-HAVEN GAZETTE and CONNECTICUT MAGA-ZINE, and may therefore conveniently be bound with it when the yearly volume is compleated. Forty-eight pages of MUSIC will be a valuable ornament to the book, and will compleat our plan of a MAGAZINE. We engage to forward the music, monthly, to such of our Customers as may choose to subscribe for it, they settling with Messieurs DOOLITTLE and READ.

MEIGS & DANA[38]

The plan and content of the musical portion was thus part of a broader conception reflecting the concerns of New Haven's artistic community. The selections were to include "the newest and most approved Pieces of Musick, both from British Authors, and American Composers," and, as the notice announced, "no Piece will be published, without being previously examined and approv'd by the *Musical Society of Yale*

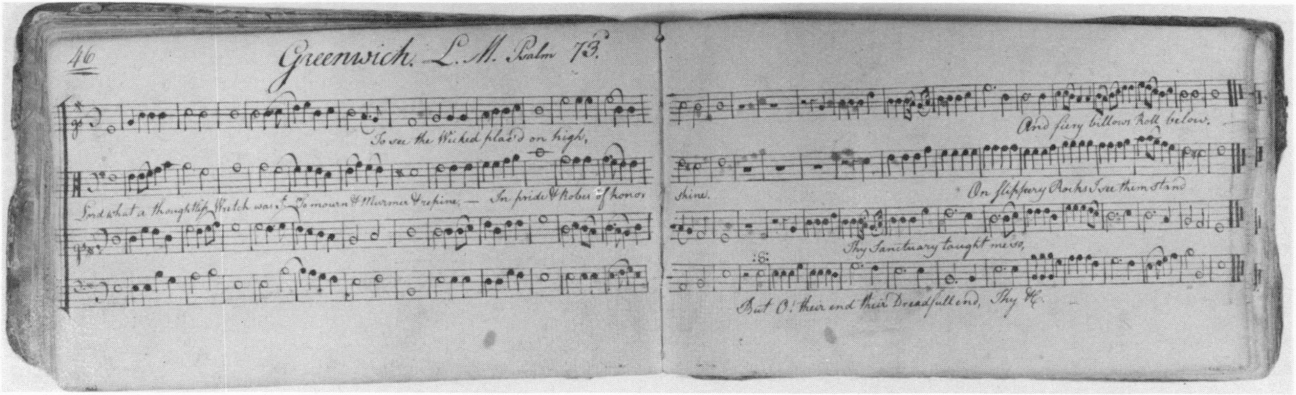

GREENWICH

Courtesy of The Hartford Seminary Foundation

College."[39] There were twenty-five tunes in four parts (12 fuges), three anthems in four parts, an "Ode for Christmas, [by Atwell] Performed in the College Chappel 1786 with universal Applaus," and five songs, four of them scored for treble and bass, and one for German flute.[40]

New Haven was part of Elihu Carpenter's working world as well, though he, like Read, grew up in Rehoboth.[41] He was a friend of Amos Doolittle and Simeon Jocelin, as an inscription in his copy of *The Chorister's Companion* suggests.[42] Eight pieces signed by Carpenter are written in manuscript in the back of the tunebook, along with Read's "Judgment," and several other hymn tunes. Carpenter's anthem, "Sing, O daughter of Zion," had the honor of being one of the three anthems (two by Billings) in *The Beauties of Psalmody* (1786), compiled for the use of the Yale Musical Society.

Musicians from other states were obviously attracted to Connecticut's centers of musical activity, but a growing number of local singing masters were heading south and west to "make their fortunes." Andrew Law, from 1782 to 1793, taught outside of Connecticut and hired an increasing number of Connecticut men to teach and sell his tune books in Virginia, Pennsylvania, and Maryland.[43] Prominent among them were Andrew Adgate (1762-1793) and Ishmail Spicer (born March 27, 1760), both from Norwich, where Law taught a singing school early in 1782.[44] Most likely both young men were his students. They probably went to Philadelphia with Law late in that year, and Adgate served as Law's assistant prior to establishing his own illustrious career. Spicer was active in Pennsylvania and Maryland and collaborated with Adgate in compiling the *Philadelphia Harmony* (1789) before returning to Connecticut about 1790.

Andrew Adgate conducted a series of famous concerts in Philadelphia, and a frequent auditor at rehearsals and performances was his friend, Noah Webster, the Connecticut lexicographer. During the years Webster travelled extensively to promote his theories and writings on the American language, he taught singing school in Baltimore, and spent part of a year teaching at the Episcopal Academy in Philadelphia. Besides singing with Adgate, Webster "read . . . [his] last lecture to 150 with great applause, closed with an anthem from Sunday Songs, tune by Mr Adgate's school."[45] Music was long a part of Webster's life, and he was especially fond of dancing, played the flute well, and taught vocal music in his home state as well as in Maryland. According to his biographer, the Webster family spent many evenings listening to older brother Abraham play the flute, and joining in singing Watts' Psalms.[46] Abraham was a chorister, and Deacon Noah Webster, Senior, read the psalm in West Society (now West Hartford) for many years.[47] Noah, Junior, attended singing school, possibly one taught by Mr. Beal in

1768 for the church. John Whitman's son, Captain Samuel, may have been there, too, since his music book is inscribed with the date 1768. Noah Webster's diary is full of musical activities, from "amusing myself with books and with a flute . . . and what a wise and happy design in the organization of the human frame that the sound of a little hollow tube of wood should dispel in a few moments, or at least alleviate, the heaviest cares of life!" to learning "a song of the Ladies, a Sweet Country Life."[48]

Webster lived in Hartford temporarily after graduation (Yale, 1778) and was a knowledgeable commentator on musical events. For example,

> [August 1, 1784, Hartford] At Church. Singing performed AM wretchedly; PM We did better.

> [September 5] Heard Mr Strong AM and Mr Boardman PM Attended public singing in the evening.

> [the 12th] At church. In the evening sang at the State house and had a large collection of people. Some from Rhode Island, &c.

> [May 29, 1785, in Baltimore] Sunday. At Mr West's church—horrible singing!

> [June 26, in Charleston, South Carolina] Pleased with the appearance of the town. Go to St. Michael's Church & hear parson Smith. Miss Storer sings Part of Handel's Oratorio—Very odd indeed! A woman sings in Public after church for her own benefit! I do not like the modern taste in singing! P.M. I go to the White meeting & Hear a little New England singing. In the evening hear a methodist.

> [April 4, 1787, in West Hartford] Public singing at West-division. Music very good.[49]

Webster advertised for a school in Baltimore in May of 1785, offering instruction in reading, speaking, writing, and "Vocal Music in as great Perfection as it is taught in America."[50] The singing school he opened in the Fall was a success, as he noted in his diary: [Sunday, September 4] Begin to sing in church; astonish all Baltimore with ten scholars; [September 7th and 8th] Great additions to my school; this is the effect produced last Sunday; [September 25th] Sunday. Fill the churches with music."[51] The school was the choir for Dr. Allison's church, and a room for instruction was probably provided. Webster charged 19s. 6d. tuition for one scholar (7s. 6d. tuition, 12s. books, 15s. for two with less for two members of the same family) and incurred weekly expenses of 30s. room and board, 3s. 9d. rent for benches, and 1s. per pound for candles. Sometimes he was paid in goods, such as a pair of shoes, stockings, or gloves.[52]

A variety of financial arrangements governed the operation of schools under the patronage of the church. Contribution money was used for Mr. Hitchcock's salary in New Haven (1787), and a portion of the general school fund, and then loan money, went towards "defraying the charge of singing" in Newington (1782).[53] The First Society in Hartford voted (1783) that "the sum of three farthings on the pound be laid on the Polls and Rateable Estate of the inhabitants," the type of plan which later came into general use in New England.[54] Some churches incurred expenses for instruments, particularly the three Episcopal churches that installed organs prior to 1789. Christ Church in Stratford was supplied with organists from the Benjamin family from the time the church resumed services in 1779.[55] Trinity Church in New Haven purchased an instrument in 1785 from London organ builder Henry Holland, and Ezra Stiles "gave Leave to Benjamin [DeLucena, possible relation of the Stratford family], a Soph., to be abs. from Chapel on Sabb. & to go to Episc° Ch[h]. till end Feb. next & play on the Organ there while Mr. Bates is learn[g] to play. But no longer."[56] Moses Bates served as organist until 1794, and his house was rent-free as compensation.[57]

Meanwhile, as financial support increased for singing schools, music expanded its official role in private academies and institutions of higher learning. The students at Plainfield Academy in Norwich, for example, were proficient enough to introduce their oratorical exhibition (1782) with music, "performed by the students and some of the gentlemen and ladies of the town . . . and an admired Latin ode, sung by the students solely, concluded the whole."[58] The School for Young Ladies in New Haven, where Jedidiah Morse was instructor until Barnabas Bidwell and Jonathan Leavitt took over in 1785, included vocal music in its curriculum. At Yale College, the traditional classical studies were supplemented by informal performance, the Musical Society, chapel services (in 1788, "the Juniors elected six singers to lead the music of the Chapel next year"[59]), and singing schools. Tutor Simeon Baldwin organized a volunteer singing school during his three-year tenure (1783-86).[60]

Under President Stiles, the arts at the college grew steadily. At the first public commencement (1781) since the beginning of the war (and the dispersal of students to several locations), an anthem "set to musick by Mr. Dwight" was sung.[61] The composer was Samuel Dwight (Yale 1773), a school teacher in New Haven. In December of 1783, Stiles "for the first time . . . admitted a Flute in Chapel with the vocal Music."[62] The Quarter Day exercises:

Music—Psalm Tune Stratford. Lat, Orat. by Prentice. 5′
Music—Poem by Col. Humphry—Tune, Washington.
Dialogue by Cone, Fowler, Hinman, Roe, 33′.
Eng. Orat. by Basset. 9′
Music—poem by Marsh a Sen. Soph. set to music by a sen[r].[63]

Another Quarter Day two years later followed a similar program.

Music vocal & instrumental III[h] 30' p.m.
Lat. Oration—Perkins I. 15 min.
    Anthem
Dialogue Griswold, Smith I,
    Hitchcock, Miller
Music instrumental behind the Curtains.
Eng. Oration. Bird. 9 min.
    Anthem.[64]

The public commencement for that year included the Sunday baccalaureate service, when "the dying Xtian to his Soul—Chapter of Job—& Reval[a] Anthem" were sung, and the ceremonies, at which the usual anthems were sung and "Handels Waterpiece p formed on a Flute closed the forenoon Exhibitions."[65]

Students could obtain instruments and music easily from New Haven merchants. Edmund Smith sold flutes and fifes, and Isaac Beers carried a wide selection, for example,

Adams's 43 Psalm Tunes and 25 Anthems
Belle's 24 easy duets for G. Fl. and Violin
Coleman's 12 Do. for Do. and Trumpet
———— Hours of Love, a collection of Sonnets for the Voice, Flute, or
    Violin.
Days of Love, four Pastoral Songs, set to Musick.
Hunting Songs set for the Voice by Handel, Boyce, and others.
Purcels' Songs, for 1, 2 or 3 Voices.
Concertos for the German Flute.

Beauties of Musick and Poetry.—Musical Magazines.—Books of Instruction for the Flute, Violin, Fife, Clarinet, and for Singing.—Vocal Inchantress. Convivial Songster.—German Flutes, both tip'd and plain. Violins.—Clarinets, Pitch Pipes, Violin Strings . . . . Jocelin's Singing Book [*Chorister's Companion*]—Read's do. [*American Singing Book*][66]

The Musical Society at Yale College was at least a year old when its activities began to be mentioned. President Stiles noted in August, 1786: "Attended in Even[g] the p form[a] of the Musical Society in Chapel"[67] The preceding winter, the Society "entertained the numerous audience in the intervals between the parts" at Quarter Day exercises.[68] In February, the following notice appeared in the *New-Haven Gazette's* advertising supplement:

"Now printing, and shortly will be ready for Sale, by AMOS DOO-LITTLE, BEAUTIES OF PSALMODY: Containing concisely the Rules of Singing, together with a Collection of the most useful and approved Psalm-Tunes and Anthems, selected by a Member of the

Musical Society of YALE-COLLEGE, as they are performed in the College-Chapel.

"These ever new, nor subject to Decay,

"Spread and grow brighter with the Length of Day—"

This Book is calculated on Purpose to furnish Schools at a much cheaper Rate than any of the Kind ever before published in America.[69]

The "Member of the *Musical Society*" was reputedly Chauncey Langdon (Yale, 1786), son of Ebenezer, Jr., of Farmington. He did not pursue a musical career after graduation, but studied law with Judge Sylvester Gilbert in Hebron. Langdon excused his anonymity by suggesting, in the preface, that honor should go to the composers and not to the editor merely for choosing between good or bad music. "His chief Design," he stated, "was to furnish the Musical Society of College not only with the Rules and Ground work of Music, but with a useful Collection of Psalm-Tunes and Anthems, which were the most approved, and the best adapted to Public and Private Worship, at a very cheap Rate."[70] The last condition was met, as the "just published" notice stated—the price was two shillings and six pence.[71]

The declared purpose of furnishing suitable music at a non-prohibitive price implied, as well, an intent to inspire correct taste by providing a standard for schools and individuals. *The Select Songster's* preface expressed similar goals.

> The design of this Publication is to furnish the Lovers of Vocal Music with a cheap Collection of elegant and approved Songs. For this Purpose considerable Labour has been used in selecting the best that are contained in the various modern Publications, in collecting a Number never before published; and in procuring the Notes. The Tunes are inserted in a plain and familiar Manner, some of them with Seconds composed for the Purpose of this Book. A few occasional Corrections have been made in the Words. A similar Liberty has been taken in altering and omitting the Symphonies and other Parts of some of the Tunes, which were originally designed for the Flute and Violin, that they might be better adapted to the Voice. Several Tunes were not to be had, but by taking them off from the Flute or Voice. These may perhaps disagree in some trivial Particulars, from the original Copies: But mistakes of this Kind, it is hoped will be pardoned; since all Things in circulating, undergo some alteration.[72]

No further elaboration would improve this succinct description of the sources of the music, in printed English collections and from oral tradition, except a reminder that cultural ties with the mother country were never severed with the decisiveness which characterizes military and political events. London was still a center of fashion, and British musicians and music continued to fulfill their traditional role in the cultural life of the new republic, as they had done throughout the colonial years.

Pride in American authorship should not be construed as rejection of British heritage. Simeon Jocelin starred with asterisks the names of American composers in *The Chorister's Companion,* and published, a few years later, *A Collection of Favorite Psalm Tunes, From late and approved British Authors.*[73] Andrew Law featured the music of London clergyman, Martin Madan (*Lock Hospital Collection,* 1769), in the revised edition of his popular *Select Harmony,* and in the process he adopted the treble-dominated texture of the charity children's choirs in British town churches.

Details of musical structure and sources, therefore, often came from British music. One of the five melodies with a new "second" in *Select Songster,* "The British Muse," dramatizes in its title its source in George F. Handel's opera, *Atalanta* (1736).[74] Handel's works, as the considered epitome of artistic excellence, were a model and a standard for American concert fare, especially after the great Handel commemoration in Westminister Abbey (1784). Daniel Read named his son George Frederick Handel Read in honor of his respect and admiration for the composer. The text for "The British Muse" was "Friendship," a poem written by Yale tutor and literary figure, Barnabas Bidwell (Yale, 1785). Bidwell was the author, as well, of the esteemed play, *The Mercenary Match.*

The eighties witnessed the beginning of professional theater in Connecticut, though plays and other entertainments had been part of "the scene" for a long while. The *American Mercury* advertised, in summer of 1788:

By Permission.

Entertainment.

Mr. Smith respectfully informs the Ladies & Gentlemen of the Place, that on this, and Wednesday and Friday evenings next, at Mr. Frederick Bull's will be delivered a series of elegant

Dramatic Speaking,

ALSO—a variety of Songs and Musical Dialogues,
A copy of which may be seen at Mr. Bull's. The whole selected from the most distinguished Poets, and

Designed to *shew* Virtue *her own Feature!*
Vice *her own Image!*
And the very Age its Form and Pressure!

Tickets one shilling and six-pence each. May be had at the Place of Performance.

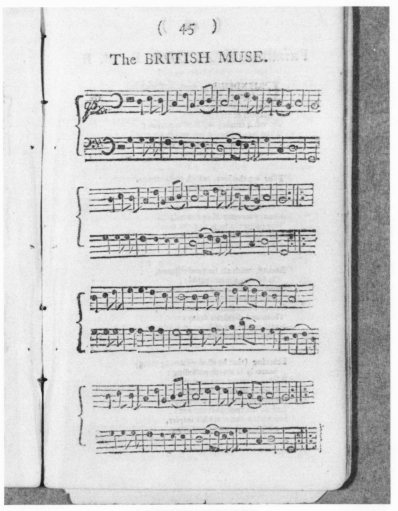

THE BRITISH MUSE

Courtesy of American Antiquarian Society

To begin at 8 o'clock exactly.

N.B. The strictest Decorum will be observed, but no Person can be admitted without a ticket.[75]

Despite the restrictive laws, public performances signified changing attitudes towards the place of the arts in the scale of social values, and urbanization helped to create audiences. (Incorporated as cities in 1784 were New Haven, Hartford, Middletown, Norwich, New London, and in the next year, East Haven, Hamden, Woodbridge [Amity], and North Haven.)

In the winter season 1788-1789, the Bull's "noted stand, fronting Court Square," in Hartford, was again the scene of both classical dramas and new ones, such as Harvard graduate (1776) Royall Tyler's popular five-act comedy, *The Contrast*. Newspaper notices appeared in the *American Mercury*:

(By Permission.)

On this evening (Monday) at Mr. FREDERICK BULL'S, will be perform'd, some very favorite scenes from Mr. Molier's Comedy of the MISER; With the almost *entire* Musical entertainment, Virgin Unmask'd, or AN Old Man taught Wisdom; with the Original SONGS, Prologues, Epilogues, &c. Tickets one quarter Dollar each—may be had at Mr. Frederick Bull's, and *no where else*. To begin at 7 o'clock exactly.

N.B. Mr. SMITH assures the Ladies and Gentlemen who may honor him with their company, that nothing in his power will be wanting to give universal satisfaction.

On Tuesday evening will be perform'd some scenes from HAMLET, Prince of Denmark; And the Farce Mayor of Garratt. SINGING as usual. Being the *last night*.[76]

An ATTIC ENTERTAINMENT
(By Authority.)

At Mr. David Bull's long Room, on Tuesday evening the 20th inst. Mr. McPherson proposes to deliver A Lecture of Heads,
(written by Geo. A. Stevens) with additions by the Lecturer; and
An Occasional PROLOGUE.
Also—Two Scenes from the Comedy of The Contrast,
Written (letely) by a Citizen of Boston.
In the course of the Lecture Thirteen Heads will be Exhibited—among'st which, The Head of An American Soldier and Patriot will be contrasted with ALEXANDER the GREAT.
To begin precisely at 6 o'clock. Tickets at one shilling and six pence each, may be had at E. Babcock's Printing Office, and at the place of performance.
NB Children at half price.

Vivat Republica.[77]

In the May 29, 1789, issue of the *Norwich Packet,* Mr. Trumbull complied with a request, "Please to insert in your paper the inclos'd, and you will oblige a number of your Country Customers.

A NEW SONG.

COME, now with joy ye blooming fair,
　And join the fed'ral throng;
Let industry attend the choir,
　Your beauties to prolong.

Since peace has blest this happy land,
　And government succeeds;
Let virtue ever take command,
　Of all your future deeds.[78]

Notes

CHAPTER I

1. Timothy Woodbridge, *The Duty of GOD's Professing People, in Glorifying their Heavenly Father; . . .* (New London, 1727), i.

2. David P. McKay and Richard Crawford, *William Billings of Boston* (Princeton, 1975), 24.

3. See Richard L. Bushman, *From Puritan to Yankee* (New York, 1970).

4. Woodbridge, *The Duty*, i.

5. *Ibid.*, ii.

6. [Thomas Clap], Some Considerations tending to put an end to the Differences that have been about Singing. Beinecke Rare Book and Manuscript Library, Yale University, New Haven.

7. *Ibid.*

8. *Ibid.*

9. See Allen P. Britton, "Theoretical Introductions in American Tunebooks to 1800" (Ph.D. dissertation, University of Michigan, 1949), 84-88, and Gilbert Chase, *America's Music* (New York, 1966), 22-40.

10. Nathaniel Chauncey, *Regular Singing Defended . . .* (New London, 1728), 46.

11. *Ibid.*, 44.

12. Ezra Stiles, *Literary Diary of Ezra Stiles, President of Yale College,* ed. Franklin B. Dexter (3 Vols., New York, 1901), I, 246.

13. J. Vicars, *Gods arke overtopping the worlds waves* (1646), quoted in Peter Le Huray, *Music and the Reformation in England, 1549-1660* (London, 1967), 54.

14. [Clap], Some Considerations.

15. See Nicholas Temperley, "Psalms, Metrical: England," in the new *Grove Dictionary of Music and Musicians* (London, 1979).

16. See Louis Benson, *The English Hymn* (New York, 1915), for an authoritative study of the development and use of hymns.

17. Jean Calvin, Foreward to *Geneva Psalter* (1543), translated in Oliver Strunk, *Source Readings in Music History* (5 Vols., New York, 1965), II, 155-158.

18. Benson, *English Hymn*, 46.

19. The parish church tradition is summarized in Nicholas Temperley, "Psalmody: England," in *Grove*. The first detailed study of parish church music is Temperley, *The Music of the English Parish Church* (2 Vols., Cambridge, England, 1979). The term "Psalmody" was first associated with the chanting of prose psalms, then with metrical psalm singing. It is now used in a broader sense to describe the practice of Protestant vocal music in America from colonial days to the early nineteenth century. See Richard Crawford, "Psalmody: American," and Nicholas Temperley, "Psalms, Metrical: America," in *Grove*.

20. [Clap], Some Considerations.

21. See Temperley, "Psalms, Metrical: America," and Irving Lowens, "The Bay Psalm Book in 17th-Century New England," *Music and Musicians in Early America* (New York, 1964), 33-35.

22. Nicholas Temperley, "John Playford and the Metrical Psalms," *Journal of the American Musicological Society*, XXV (Fall, 1972), 331.

23. Nicholas Temperley, "The Anglican Communion Hymn, Part I, Hymn Singing in the Church of England: Tradition and the Law," *The Hymn*, 30 (January 1979), 9.

24. Records of the First Church of Christ, New Haven, Supplement to Vol. 2, 74, Mss. Record Group 70, The Connecticut State Library, Hartford. The entry states: "The Church by their Vote signifyed their approbation and Desire that Watts's Psalms be used commonly in their Worship, instead of the Old Version of the Psalms." (February 3, 1762).

25. Ezra Stiles, *Extracts from the Itineraries and Other Miscellanies of Ezra Stiles, 1755-1774*, ed. Franklin B. Dexter (New Haven, 1916), 140.

26. John Cotton, *Singing of Psalmes a Gospel-Ordinance* (London, 1647), 62.

27. Ashford Records, entry September 6, 1721, quoted in Ellen D. Larned, *History of Windham County, Connecticut* (2 Vols., Worcester, 1874), I, 230.

28. New London Town Records, entry January 13, 1723/24, quoted in Frances M. Caulkins, *History of New London* (2nd Ed., New London, 1860), 379.

29. Farmington: Abstracts from Town Meeting Records, 304, Genealogical Mss., The Connecticut Historical Society, Hartford.

30. Oscar Zeichner, *Connecticut's Years of Controversy 1750-1776* (Williamsburg, 1949), 220.

31. As Alan P. Merriam points out in Chapter VII of *The Anthropology of Music* (Evanston, 1964), "If every group holds the music abilities of some of its members to be greater than that of others, it follows that in some groups such individuals must stand out more sharply than in others. Here we begin to approach professionalism, which is usually defined in terms of whether the musician is paid for and supported economically by his skill. . . . There must be a number of degrees of professionalism; . . . it is difficult to know at what point professionalism begins and ends . . . ." 124-25.

32. Records of the First Congregational Society, Woodstock, Vol. I, Church Meetings 1728-1826, Mss. Record Group 70, The Connecticut State Library, Hartford.

33. Records of the First Ecclesiastical Society of West Hartford, 1736-1782, Mss. Record Group 70, The Connecticut State Library, Hartford.

34. Freeman W. Meyer, *Connecticut Congregationalism in the Revolutionary Era* (Hartford, 1977), 15.

35. Charles M. Andrews, *The Beginnings of Connecticut 1632-1662* (New Haven, 1933), 18.

36. Enfield's Town Book of Four Acts and Voats of the Town beginning from y° 1693 to y° 1700, in Francis O. Allen, *The History of Enfield, Connecticut* (3 Vols., Lancaster, Pennsylvania, 1900), I, 296.

37. Henry R. Stiles, *The History and Genealogies of Ancient Windsor, Connecticut* (2 Vols., Hartford, 1892/1976 reprint), I, 273-74.

38. *Ibid.*, 274.

39. Records of the First Ecclesiastical Society of West Hartford.

40. See William H. Tallmadge, "Baptist Monophonic and Heterophonic Hymnody in Southern Appalachia," *Yearbook for Inter-American Musical Research*, XI (1975), 106-36.

41. Quoted in Henry W. Foote, *Three Centuries of American Hymnody* (Cambridge, Massachusetts, 1940), 376.

42. Nicholas Temperley, "The Old Way of Singing: Its Origins and Development," unpublished paper delivered at the conference on Rural Hymnody at Berea College, Berea, Kentucky, April 1979, used with permission of the author.

43. Chauncey, *Regular Singing*, 43, 48.

44. Tune collected in Strathpeffer in Ross-shire by Joseph Mainzer and printed in *Gaelic Psalm-tunes* (Edinburgh, 1846), as quoted by John S. Curwen, *Studies in Worship Music, First Series* (London, [1880]), 72.

45. Britton, "Theoretical Introductions," 87.

46. Willi Apel, *Harvard Dictionary of Music* (2nd Ed., Cambridge, Massachusetts, 1972), 70.

47. Leslie Shepard, *The History of Street Literature* (Detroit, 1977), 21.

48. *Connecticut Courant*, May 27, 1765.

49. Chauncey, *Regular Singing*, 48.

50. Thomas Symmes, *The Reasonableness of Regular Singing* (Boston, 1720), quoted in Britton, "Theoretical Introductions," 85.

51. [Clap], Some Considerations.

52. Alan Lomax, *Folk Song Style and Culture* (New Brunswick, 1978), 8.

53. Woodbridge, *The Duty*, iv.

54. Town meeting minutes, in Charles H. Davis, *History of Wallingford, Connecticut* (Meriden, 1870), 404.

55. *History of the Congregational Church, 150th Anniversary, Columbia* (Hartford, 1867), 49.

56. Alonzo B. Chapin, *Glastonbury for Two Hundred Years* (Hartford 1853), 77.

57. The Hartford Association was one of the centralized bodies created by the Saybrook Platform of 1707. The first four associations were Hartford North, Hartford South, Fairfield, and New Haven.

58. Records of the First Church of Christ, Hartford, 1684-1930, 35, Mss. Record Group 70, The Connecticut State Library, Hartford.

59. *Ibid.*, 36.

60. Records of the Farmington First Society, quoted in David N. Camp, *History of New Britain, 1640-1889* (New Britain, 1889), 87.

61. Printed in Julius Gay, *Farmington Papers* (Privately printed, 1929), 36.

62. Bella tune from John Tufts, *A Very Plain and Easy Introduction to the Singing of Psalm Tunes* (Boston, 1723, 3rd Ed.), 3, and Cambridge short tune from Playford (1671) in Maurice Frost, *English & Scottish Psalm & Hymn Tunes* (London, 1953), Frost No. 154a, 187.

63. Josiah Dwight, *An Essay to Silence the Outcry that Has Been Made in Some Places against Regular Singing* (Boston, 1725), 11.

64. Farmington: Abstracts, 233. The Church, in this period, referred to only the select group of covenanted members; the Society included a larger membership of male rate-payers in the area served by one meeting house.

65. Records of East Windsor Society, quoted in Stiles, *Windsor*, I, 565. Edwards kept abreast of the latest developments in the Regular Singing movement. His account book entry: "Sept 13. [1728] I had of him [Deacon Skinner] Mr Chauncey's Book of Regular Singing wch as I rembr: he told me was 16d," Folio Account Book, first leaf, verso, Beinecke Rare Book and Manuscript Library, Yale University, New Haven.

66. John A. Stoughton, *Windsor Farmes, A Glimpse of an Old Parish* (Hartford, 1883), 97.

67. Mary Beale Kenyon, "George and Matthew Beale: English Singing Masters in Connecticut, 1727-1773," Unpublished paper, courtesy of the author. Mrs. Kenyon believes that a letter written by Jonathan Edwards, from Windsor, may have been directed to George Beale, then living in Deerfield. The letter asks the recipient to come to Stockbridge "to teach the Indians to sing. They have good voices and many of them are apt to learn and I should be glad if I could get you there the next Fall or winter to that End if you could be obtained on reasonable terms. I desire that you would inform me whether you would be willing to come and on what terms . . . Your pay will be good . . . . I suppose

you would expect to be paid not only for the time you should spend at Stockbridge but for your journey at least in part but perhaps you might afford to come if we should pay your journey from Westfield. It might not be out of your way to come as far as Westfield or Springfield on your own Business, it being on your way to Deerfield." Jonathan Edwards to unidentified correspondent, June 4, 1753, Betts Autograph Collection, Mss. and Archives, Yale University Library, New Haven.

68. George Beale will and inventory, April, 1761, Probate Book 1, 68ff., Town Hall, Stafford Springs, Connecticut, Facsimile courtesy of Mary Beale Kenyon.

69. Alan C. Buechner, "Yankee Singing Schools and the Golden Age of Choral Music in New England, 1760-1800" (Ed.D. dissertation, Harvard University, 1959), 139.

70. *Ibid.*, 91-101. Buechner discusses in detail the Harvard music curriculum.

71. See Note 81.

72. Yale College, *Theses & Quaestiones 1702-1797* (New Haven).

73. See Buechner, "Singing Schools," 99.

74. Latin theses were translated and interpreted by Dr. Alma C. Browne, Urbana, Illinois.

75. Apel, *Harvard Dictionary*, 709.

76. Ezra Stiles, College Notebook, December 28, 1749, Ezra Stiles Papers, Microfilm edition reel 13:89, Beinecke Rare Book and Manuscript Library, Yale University, New Haven.

77. *Ibid.*, April 20, 1745, reel 13:45.

78. According to William H. Wilcoxson, *History of Stratford* (Stratford, 1939), 283, training days began with religious ceremony. The format of other public occasions would seem to support his observation, but he did not include documentary evidence.

79. Franklin B. Dexter, *Biographical Sketches of the Graduates of Yale College with Annals of the College History* (6 Vols., New York, 1855-1912), I, 178.

80. John Sargeant, *A Valedictorian Oration, by John Sargeant, delivered at Yale College in the Year 1729* (New York, 1882), 30. The original manuscript is at Williams College.

81. Samuel Whittelsey to Nathaniel Chauncey, printed in the Appendix to William C. Fowler, *Memorials of the Chaunceys* (Boston, 1858), 277-278, states: "[Wallingford, March 25, 1727] . . . if you will come along on Tuesday morning next . . . I will promise to go with you [to New Haven] . . . The Rector is a great friend to Regular Singing; so you may have an opportunity upon y^t acct."

82. Cotton Mather, *Manuductio ad Ministerium, Directions for a Candidate* . . . (Boston, 1726) quoted in Buechner," Yankee Singing Schools," 101.

83. John Cleaveland, Diary, January 15, 1741/2—May 11, 1742, Facsimile of the Manuscript, Mss. and Archives, Yale University Library, New Haven.

84. An effort to introduce Anglican religious societies was made by the Society for the Propagation of the Gospel. In Boston, one was founded in 1704. (William Perry, *Historical Collections Relating to the American Colonial Church*, Hartford, 1873, III, 76-9.) Information in Mason Martens, "Tate and Brady's New Version of the Metrical Psalms and its Introduction into the American Colonies," Unpublished paper delivered at the American Musicological Society meeting, Washington, 1976. Cited in Temperley, "The Old Way."

85. The Donation of the Reverend Isaac Watts, D.D., of London to Yale College Library, 1730, Beinecke Rare Book and Manuscript Library, Yale University, New Haven.

86. Richard Crawford, "Watts for Singing: Metrical Poetry in American Sacred Tunebooks, 1761-1785," *Journal of Early American Literature*, XI (1976), 140.

87. Benson, *The English Hymn*, 111.

88. *Ibid.* Two important versions of Watts were Joel Barlow's "Corrected and Enlarged" edition, published in Hartford in 1785, and Timothy Dwight's edition, also published in Hartford, in 1801.

89. Records of the First Ecclesiastical Society, West Hartford. Italics Mine.

90. Jacob Eliot, Diary, March 28, 1742, Eliot Family Papers, Mss. and Archives, Yale University Library, New Haven.

91. Joseph Tracy, *The Great Awakening* (Boston, 1842), 202.

92. Letter from Elisha Paine, July 3, 1744, printed in Isaac Backus, *A History of New England with Particular Reference to the Denomination of Christians called Baptists* (2 Vols., Newton, Massachusetts, 1871), II, 67.

93. Tracy, *Great Awakening*, 242.

94. *Diary of the Reverend Daniel Wadsworth*, Notes by George Walker (Hartford, 1894), 30.

95. John A. Stoughton, *Windsor Farmes*, 51.

96. Frances M. Caulkins, *History of Norwich* (Hartford, 1866), 332.

97. Oscar G. Sonneck, *Early Concert-Life in America* (Leipzig, 1907), 7.

98. Franklin B. Dexter, Editor, *Ancient Town Records* (3 Vols., New Haven, 1917), II, 28.

99. *Ibid.*, 25

100. *The English Dancing Master* (thereafter titled *The Dancing Master*) went through 23 editions between 1650 and 1728. See Margeret Dean-Smith, *Playford's English Dancing Master, 1651* (London, 1957).

101. Jew's harps were valuable enough to be listed individually in personal inventories and by the dozens in inventories of merchants and traders; for example, Thomas Fenner, 1647 (Charles W. Manwaring, *Digest of the Early Connecticut Probate Records*, 3 Vols., Hartford, 1904-6, I, 11.) and goldsmith Rene Grignon (Norwich Probate Records, 1715, Number 2317). It should be noted that Peters' supposed Blue Law prohibiting instrumental music exempted the three most common instruments, namely, the drum, trumpet, and Jew's harp.

102. Broadside, Julian Marshall Collection, Houghton Library, Harvard University, Cambridge.

103. Kate Van Winkle Keller and Carolyn Rabson, *National Tune Index* (to be published by University Music Editions, New York). The index is a computerized data bank of information on about 40,000 songs and tunes in the Anglo-American popular music repertory.

104. Christopher French, Journal, Vol. 3, Book 4, September 19, 1776 entry, Manuscripts Division, Library of Congress, Washington.

105. *Giles Gibbs, Jr. His Book for the Fife*, ed. Kate Van Winkle Keller (Hartford, 1974), 11.

106. Sonneck, *Concert-Life*, 9, and Note 68.

107. James Morris, *A Statistical Account of Several Towns in the County of Litchfield* (New Haven, 1815), 97.

108. *Connecticut Courant*, July 11, 1780. Simeon Baldwin's niece wrote the following P.S. in her letter of December 3, 1783, from Norwich: "Bristo sends his duty And ses he learns to fiddle bravely. He is to fiddle to Aunt Molly's

wedding." (Simeon E. Baldwin, *Life and Letters of Simeon Baldwin*, New Haven, 1919), 7.

109. Will and Inventory of Abda Duce, 1708/9, Hartford Probate Records, The Connecticut State Library, Hartford.

110. Frederick C. Norton, "Negro Slavery in Connecticut," *Connecticut Magazine*, V (1899), 323.

111. Inventory of John Livingston, 1721, Number 3238, New London Probate Records, The Connecticut State Library, Hartford. He was a military man and the son-in-law of diarist Madame Sarah Knight.

112. Inventory of John Benjamin, 1773, Number 655, and Inventory of John Benjamin, Jr., 1796, Number 211, Stratford Probate Records, The Connecticut State Library, Hartford.

113. Baldwin, *Life and Letters*, 203.

114. Caulkins, *New London*, 110.

115. Stiles, *Windsor*, I, 184.

116. *Ibid.*, 185.

117. Dexter, *Ancient Town Records*, I, 48.

118. *Ibid.*, I, 175.

119. Manwaring, *Probate Records*, II, 491.

120. Dexter, *Ancient Town Records*, I, 237.

121. *Ibid.*, back of Vol. I.

122. *Ibid.*, I, 474.

123. *Ibid.*, I, 480.

124. *Public Records of the State of Connecticut* (10 Vols., Hartford, 1894-1965), I, 542.

125. *Ibid.*, I, 543.

126. Raoul F. Camus, "The Military Band in the United States Army Prior to 1834" (Ph.D. dissertation, New York University, 1969), 27.

127. *Ibid.*

128. *Ibid.*, 104.

129. *Ibid.*, 34.

130. *Ibid.*

131. Condensed from Camus, 34-35, where the duty calls are paraphrased from Bariffe, *Military Discipline, or the Young Artillery Man* (1643).

132. Joshua Hempstead, *Diary, Collections of the New London County Historical Society*, I (1901), 147.

133. Caulkins, *New London*, 197.

134. Town Records, 1, 18, quoted in Wilcoxson, *Stratford*, 141.

135. Town Records, I, 31, quoted in Stiles, *Windsor*, I, 176.

CHAPTER II

1. Carl Bridenbaugh, *Cities in Revolt* (New York, 1971), 5.

2. *Ibid.*

3. *Ibid.*, 263.

4. New Haven *Connecticut Gazette*, December 6, 1760.

5. *Connecticut Courant*, December 10, 1764.

6. *Ibid.*, May 26, 1766.

7. Bridenbaugh, *Cities*, 263.

8. John Adams, *Diary and Autobiography*, ed. L.H. Butterfield (4 Vols., Cambridge, Massachusetts, 1961), II, 30.

9. *The New York Gazette*, January 14, 1760, in Sonneck, *Concert-Life*, 163.

10. Sonneck, *Concert-Life*, 163.

11. New Haven *Connecticut Gazette*, July 26, 1760.

12. New London *Connecticut Gazette*, September 25, 1767.

13. *New London Summary*, June 11, 1762.

14. Adams, *Diary*, II, 24.

15. *Ibid.*, 30.

16. Volumes 1 and 2 were published in 1729, 3 and 4 in 1730, and 5 and 6 in 1731. Another popular collection was the *British Musical Miscellany, or the Delightful Grove. Being a collection of celebrated English and Scotch Songs* (6 Vols., London, 1734-36).

17. New London *Connecticut Gazette*, August 19, 1768.

18. Josiah Flagg was a Massachusetts musician, active in promoting concerts, training militia band musicians, and publishing music collections. The *Collection of the Best Psalm Tunes* (Boston, 1764) and *Sixteen Anthems* (Boston, 1766) were compilations containing "modern" music from the British Psalmody school.

19. *Connecticut Courant*, November, 1769.

20. *New London Summary*, February 16, 1759.

21. *Ibid.*, May 15, 1761.

22. New London *Connecticut Gazette*, July 22, 1768.

23. Dickinson wrote to James Otis, "I enclose you a song for American freedom. I have long since renounced poetry, but as indifferent songs are frequently very powerful on certain occasions, I venture to invoke the deserted muses. . . ." Quoted in James C. Gaston. "An Anthology of Poems dealing with the American Revolution taken from prominent London Magazines and Newspapers, 1763-1783" (Ph.D. dissertation, University of Oklahoma, 1975), 9.

24. Arthur Schrader, "Songs to Cultivate the Sensations of Freedom," *Music in Colonial Massachusetts*, ed. Barbara Lambert, (Boston, in press).

25. "Heart of Oak," S186, Claude Simpson, *The British Broadside Ballad and its Music* (New Brunswick, 1966), 300. Simpson points out that the "s" on the word Hearts was not there originally, but has been added through popular use.

26. "Liberty Song" from the New London *Connecticut Gazette*, July 22, 1768. 'Hearts of Oak" from William Chappell, *The Ballad Literature and Popular Music of the Olden Time* (2 Vols., New York, Dover reprint, 1965), II, 716.

27. Arthur Schrader, *Songs Under the Liberty Tree* (in preparation).

28. A broadside edition was advertised in the August 29, 1768, *Boston Chronicle*, but no copy seems to have survived. See Vera B. Lawrence, *Music for Patriots, Politicians, and Presidents* (New York, 1975), 27. The song was printed with words and music in *Bickerstaff's Boston Almanac for 1769*. See also Carolyn Rabson, *Songbook of the American Revolution* (Peaks Island, Maine, 1974), 93. Rabson includes four songs to the tune "Hearts of Oak."

29. "Vicar of Bray", S488, Simpson, *British Broadside*, 738.

30. "Observations on the Several Commanders of the Ship Connecticut," Trumbull Papers, The Connecticut Historical Society, Hartford.

31. "The Vicar of Bray Set for German Flute," [London, ca.1750], British Library, London.

32. Mather Byles to Polley Byles, February 18, 1768, Byles Family Papers, 1753-1865, The Massachusetts Historical Society, Boston.

33. Summary in Lawrence, *Music*, 28.

34. New London *Connecticut Gazette*, August 19, 1768.

35. *Boston Evening-Post*, June 26, 1769, quoted in Lawrence, *Music*, 29.

36. *Connecticut Courant*, September 25, 1769.

37. *Ibid.*

38. [Benjamin Trumbull], Rules for Singing, Commonplace Book HM 13717, The Huntington Library, San Marino, California, 120, reproduced by permission. A photostatic copy is in Mss. and Archives, Yale University Library, New Haven.

39. John Rowe, *Diary*, ed. Edward L. Pierce, quoted in Sonneck, *Concert-Life*, 321-22.

40. Adams, *Diary*, II, 32.

41. Samuel B. Webb to Sally Webb, November 21, 1772, Samuel Blatchley Webb Papers, Mss. and Archives, Yale University Library, New Haven.

42. Mary G. Powell, Editor, "A Scotchman's Journey in New England in 1771," *New England Magazine*, XII (May, 1895), 351.

43. *Connecticut Courant*, June 13, 1766.

44. John Trumbull, *An Essay on the Use and Advantages of the Fine Arts delivered at the Public Commencement in New-Haven. September 12th. 1770.* (New Haven: T. and S. Green), 14.

45. Stiles, *Diary*, III, 14-15.

46. Julian Mates, *The American Musical Stage Before 1800* (New Brunswick, 1962), 183 and Chapter V.

47. New London *Connecticut Gazette*, August 27, 1773. A pictorial satire and interpretation can be found in Mary D. George, *Catalogue of Political and Personal Satire* (London, 1935), V, 112-15, Prints 5106, 5109, and 5110.

48. Dexter, *Biographical Sketches and Annals*, II, 7.

49. "History of the New Haven Theater: 18th Century," 10-13, Theatre Mss. Collection, Mss. and Archives, Yale University Library, New Haven.

50. *Ibid.*, 13.

51. The Minutes of the Meetings of the Linonian Society of Yale College, 20, Photostatic copy of Records, Records of the Old Library, Yale University Archives, Yale University Library, New Haven.

52. Edith B. Schnapper, *The British Union-Catalogue of Early Music* (2 Vols., London, 1957), I, 387, 446; II, 1023.

53. Stiles, *Diary*, II, 325.

54. James Hillhouse to Nathan Hale, July 11, 1774, quoted in Mates, *Musical Stage*, 44.

55. *Connecticut Courant*, September 25, 1769.

56. Nathan H. Allen, Music in a New England State: From Psalmody to Symphony in Connecticut, 62, Watkinson Library, Trinity College, Hartford. Allen's book-length manuscript was completed before his death in 1925, but was never published.

57. *Ibid.*, 61.

58. Solomon Drowne, Diary, April 20, 1772, quoted in Richard Crawford, *Andrew Law, American Psalmodist* (Evanston, 1968), 6.

59. Biographical information from Amos Bull file, The Connecticut Historical Commission, Hartford.

60. New Haven *Connecticut Gazette*, November 29, 1766.

61. The Middletown organ gift was reported in Maurer Maurer, "Colonial Organs and Organists as Research Subject," *The Diapason*, 48 (March 1957), 24-25. Unfortunately, Maurer does not footnote his information, and a preliminary search of the Alsop Family Papers in Mss. and Archives, Yale University

Library, did not reveal the source. The Stratford organ subscription is reported in Samuel Orcutt, *A History of the Old Town of Stratford and the City of Bridgeport, Connecticut* (3 Vols., New Haven, 1886), I, 354-55.

62. Records of the First Congregational Church, Middletown, Series 2, Vol. 3 (1732-1805), 20, Record Group 70, The Connecticut State Library, Hartford.

63. Amos Bull to Samuel Smith, January 12, 1772, Julius Gay Manuscripts, The Connecticut Historical Society, Hartford.

64. *Ibid.*

65. Records of the Church of the Holy Trinity, Middletown, Meetings and Vital Records, 13, Record Group 70, The Connecticut State Library, Hartford.

66. New London *Connecticut Gazette*, September 9, 1774.

67. *Norwich Packet*, February 16, 1775.

68. See Buechner, "Yankee Singing Schools," and McKay and Crawford, *William Billings*, Chapter 1.

69. Benjamin Trumbull, Book of Accompts [1755-58], Benjamin Trumbull Papers, Mss. and Archives, Yale University Library, New Haven.

70. Psalm tunes in diamond notes comprise the music in the first pages of singing books compiled by Benjamin Trumbull, Samuel Whitman, Susanna Miles, and Deacon Story, to name a few.

71. Samuel Whitman, His Book, 1768, *The Gamut or Scale of Musick*, Whitman Papers, Box 2, The Connecticut Historical Society, reproduced with permission.

72. Susanna Miles, Her Singing Book, Anno Domini 1759, Beinecke Rare Book and Manuscript Library, Yale University, New Haven, reproduced with permission.

73. See Leslie Shepard, *Street Literature*, Chapter 1.

74. *Connecticut Courant*, February 11, 1788.

75. Enodias Bidwell, Pen Work commonplace book, 1772, East Hartford, Mss. Collection, The Connecticut Historical Society, Hartford.

76. Jesse Rogers, Commonplace book (music), Watkinson Library, Trinity College, Hartford. The manuscript contains entries from 1712 to ca.1795.

77. *Connecticut Courant*, March 25, 1765. The advertisement appears in facsimile in J. William Frost, *Connecticut Education in the Revolutionary Era* V (Chester, Conn., 1974), 33.

78. James D. McCallum, *Eleazar Wheelock, Founder of Dartmouth College* (Hanover, 1939), 88.

79. Thomas Knibb to Samson Occom, February 8, 1768, Samson Occom Papers, The Connecticut Historical Society, Hartford.

80. Eliot to Wheelock, May 18, 1764, quoted in McCallum, *Wheelock*, 87. It should be noted that Connecticut's Indians had their own traditional musical culture, but this study of the State's musical life does not allow sufficient room for adequate discussion.

81. Eleazar Wheelock, Minutes and Journal, 1761-62, Wheelock Papers, Dartmouth College, Hanover, New Hampshire; Microfilm reel 13, The Connecticut State Library, Hartford.

82. David Fowler to Eleazar Wheelock, June 15, 1765, quoted in Eleazar Wheelock, *A Brief Narrative of the Indian Charity-School in Lebanon in Connecticut, New England* (London, 1767), 38.

83. Samuel Kirtland to Eleazar Wheelock, January 22, 1765, quoted in *Ibid.*, 35.

84. Eleazar Wheelock to Nathaniel Whitaker, April 11, 1767, Wheelock Papers, Microfilm, no. 767261.4 in correspondence.

85. Joseph Johnson, Diary, Manuscripts Division, New York Public Library, New York.

86. Records of the First Congregational Church, Woodstock, Box 98, 173, Record Group 70:47, The Connecticut State Library, Hartford.

87. *Ibid.*

88. *Ibid.*

89. Adams, *Diary*, II, 31. Italics Mine.

90. Records of the First Congregational Church, East Hartford (originally Hartford Third Society), Record Group 70, The Connecticut State Library, Hartford.

91. Records of First Ecclesiastical Society, Litchfield, Vol. I, Meetings 1768-1829, entry dated April 7, 1774, The Connecticut State Library, Hartford.

92. Records, Middletown (See Note 62), entry of December 10, 1771.

93. United Church Records, Vol. III, 46, RG 70, The Connecticut State Library, Hartford.

94. *Ibid.*, 68.

95. Benjamin Trumbull Papers, North Haven Folder, Mss. and Archives, Yale University Library.

96. Benjamin Trumbull, Notes on Psalmody on verso of letter to Chauncy Whittelsey, November 30, 1768, Benjamin Trumbull Papers.

97. *Connecticut Courant*, May 7, 1771.

98. *The Public Records of the Colony of Connecticut*, ed. Charles J. Hoadly, XIII, 190.

99. Isaac Stiles, *The Character and Duty of Soldiers* (New Haven, 1755), 7.

100. Raoul Camus, *Military Music of the American Revolution* (Chapel Hill, 1976), 16.

101. Fife tutors in use in England and America, for example; *The Compleat Tutor for the Fife, Containing easy Rules for Learners after a New Method* (London: David Rutherford, ca.1756) and *The Compleat Tutor for the Fife: Containing the best & easiest instructions to learn that instrument, with a collection of celebrated march's & airs performed in the Guards, & other regiments, &c.* (London: Thompson & Son, ca.1759).

102. Isaac Greenwood, Editor, *The Revolutionary Service of John Greenwood* (New York, 1922), 4.

103. New Haven *Connecticut Gazette*, November 28, 1761.

104. *Ibid.*, November 28, 1767.

105. *Connecticut Courant*, July 6, 1764.

106. Camus, *Military Music*, 19.

107. *Boston Chronicle*, June 26/29, 1769, quoted in Sonneck, *Concert-Life*, 261.

108. Simpson, *British Broadside*, 13.

109. "The British Grenadier: Together with The Grenadier's March, and an excellent new Song on the Year Fifty-Nine," New London, [ca.1760], The Connecticut Historical Society, Hartford.

110. Broadside, Julian Marshall Collection, Houghton Library, Harvard University, Cambridge, Massachusetts.

111. "The British Grenadier," (Note 109). The sheet also contains the popular song, "Lillies of France."

112. Thomas Hamelton Orderly Book, Cumberland County Historical Society, Carlisle, Pennsylvania. The regiment was raised early in 1759 for a year's service.

113. "Song on Liberty" from the *Connecticut Courant,* May 8, 1775. The text begins, "That seat of science Athens and earth's proud mistress Rome, Where now are all their glories?"

114. See Note 110. A version of the tune was adopted toward the end of the eighteenth century by the British Grenadier Guards Band, according to Chappell, *Popular Music,* I, 152, who dates the tune ca.1759.

115. *Connecticut Courant,* March 16, 1773.

116. Samuel B. Webb, *Reminiscences,* ed. James Webb (New York, 1882), 16.

CHAPTER III

1. "The American Hero. A Sapphick Ode, By Nath. Niles, A.M." Norwich, October 1775, bound with Andrew Law, *A Select Number of Plain Tunes* (Cheshire, 1781). "Bunker Hill" reproduced with permission of The Connecticut Historical Society, Hartford.

2. Albert E. Van Dusen, *Connecticut* (New York, 1961), 133.

3. *Ibid.*

4. Harry Warfel, *Noah Webster, Schoolmaster to America* (New York, 1936), 27.

5. *Record of Service of Connecticut Men,* I.–War of the Revolution (Hartford, 1889), Lexington Alarm, 19.

6. *Ibid.* 17, 25-26.

7. *Ibid.,* 5-28, and "Revolution Rolls and Lists 1775-1783," *Collections of the Connecticut Historical Society,* VIII.

8. "Moses Fargos Orderly Book for Capt William Coits Company, April 23, 1775," *Collections of the Connecticut Historical Society,* VII, 14.

9. *Ibid.,* 25-26.

10. *Orderly Book of Lieutenant Abraham Chittenden* (New Haven, 1904), entry dated August 28, 1776, 21.

11. "Fargos Orderly Book," 29.

12. Emily E. Ford, Compiler, *Notes on the Life of Noah Webster,* ed. Emily E. Skeel, (2 Vols., New York, 1912), I, 18.

13. Camus, *Military Music,* 60.

14. "Fargos Orderly Book," 41.

15. Roger Hooker, Orderly Book kept at Roxbury, May 18, 1775-September 27, 1775, entry of Thursday, July 20, Lewis Walpole Library (Yale University), Farmington.

16. "Fargos Orderly Book," July 30, 1775, 72. For a discussion of the socio-economic conditions of fifers and drummers, see Simon V. Anderson, "American Music during the War for Independence, 1775-1783" (Ph.D. dissertation, University of Michigan, 1965), Chapter II.

17. Camus, *Military Music,* 94. The facsimile is from Giles Gibbs, His Book for the Fife, 1777, reproduced with permission of The Connecticut Historical Society, Hartford. Gibbs' manuscript commonplace book preserves a repertory of military marches, duty calls, song and dance tunes, and three psalm tunes current at the beginning of the war.

18. Camus, *Military Music,* 93.

19. Ammi R. Robbins, *Journal of the Rev. Ammi R. Robbins* (New Haven, 1850), 36-7.

20. *Ibid.,* 43.

21. Chappell, *Popular Music*, II, 715.

22. Files of Kate Keller. "Lovely Nancy" is copied in Abel Joslen's and Aaron Thompson's commonplace books.

23. "The Flowers of Edinburgh, or Darling Swain," in music books of Giles Gibbs, Aaron Thompson, Nathaniel Brown, and Asa Wilcox (1793), was printed in Vol. I of *Clio and Euterpe* (London, 1758) and *The Universal Magazine* (London, 1749). It is copied in a manuscript collection bound with John Simpson's flute tutor (London, 1749). Information from Keller and Rabson, *Tune Index*.

24. "Over the Hills and Far Away," S360, was printed in *Pills* (1706), IV. 99, and was used in ten ballad operas, the most famous being Gay's *Beggar's Opera*. See Simpson, *British Broadside*, 561-63, and Bertrand Bronson, *Traditional Tunes of the Child Ballads* (4 Vols., Princeton, 1959-72), I, 14-16. Gibbs wrote out the march in his fife book, calling it "King George's March."

25. See Gibbs, His Book, 21. Students of the popular music repertory preserved in eighteenth-century manuscripts will be able to consult two works that will be published shortly by the Music Library Association. One is a detailed inventory of selected manuscripts by James Fuld and Mary Davidson; the other is a checklist of manuscripts in North American libraries by Kate Keller.

26. Penrose R. Hoopes, *Shop Records of Daniel Burnap, Clockmaker* (Hartford, 1958), 42.

27. History Workshop of the Mansfield Historical Society, *Chronology of Mansfield, Connecticut 1702-1972* (Storrs, 1974), 46.

28. Hoopes, *Shop Records*, 42.

29. *Ibid.*, 43-44. Composer Timothy Swan was one of Burnap's clock customers.

30. White was active after the war in Woodstock. See Hoopes, *Connecticut Clockmakers of the Eighteenth Century* (Hartford, 1930), 122.

31. Calvin Pease, Journal, entry August 22, 1775, American Revolution Orderly Books and Journals, Box III, The Connecticut Historical Society, Hartford.

32. *Giles Gibbs, Jr.*, Preface.

33. *Pennsylvania Gazette*, July 3, 1776, in Sonneck and Upton, *A Bibliography of Early Secular American Music* (New York, Da Capo reprint, 1964), 85. The English edition was *The Compleat Tutor for the Fife* (London, ca.1770).

34. George Willig (Philadelphia [1805]).

35. Nathaniel Morgan, "Journal," *Collections of The Connecticut Historical Society*, VII, 108.

36. Simeon Lyman, "Journal," entry October 7, 1775, *Ibid.*, 121.

37. Colonel Israel Angell, *The Diary of Colonel Israel Angell . . . 1778-1781*, ed. Edward Field (Providence, 1899), 99.

38. Robbins, *Journal*, 41.

39. Benjamin Boardman, "Diary of Rev. Benjamin Boardman," *Proceedings of the Massachusetts Historical Society*, VII (1892), 412.

40. Stiles, *Diary*, II, 483. This version was probably a choral setting such as Simeon Jocelin printed in the second edition of *The Chorister's Companion* (1788). The facsimile from Gibbs, His Book, is reproduced with permission of The Connecticut Historical Society.

41. James Oswald, *Caledonian Pocket Companion* (12 Vols., London, 1745-60), IV, 3. The facsimile from Aaron Thompson, Book of Music, is reproduced with permission of Mss. and Archives, Yale University Library, New Haven.

42. Camus, *Military Music,* 116-117.

43. Robbins, *Journal,* 41.

44. Ammi R. Robbins to Philemon and Hannah Robbins, April 9, 1776, A.R. and P. Robbins Correspondence and Papers, Folder 1742-1792, The Connecticut Historical Society, Hartford.

45. Pease, Journal, August 17, 1775; Lyman, "Journal," *Collections of The Connecticut Historical Society,* VII, 113.

46. John Trumbull, *M'Fingal: A Modern Epic Poem, in Four Cantos* (Hartford, 1782), Canto third, 66.

47. Camus, *Military Music,* 129.

48. *Ibid.,* 130-31.

49. *Connecticut Courant,* October 13, 1778.

50. *Ibid.,* February 3, 1777.

51. Samuel B. Webb, Accounts—Contra 1777, Vol. I (A), 89, Samuel Blatchley Webb Papers, Mss. and Archives, Yale University Library, New Haven.

52. James Bremner to Richard Peters, June 22, 1779, quoted in Camus, *Military Music,* 135-36.

53. *Ibid.*

54. Benjamin Trumbull, Journal, July 25, 1775, American Revolution Journals and Orderly Books, Box III, The Connecticut Historical Society, Hartford.

55. Camus, *Military Music,* 74.

56. Ebenezer Huntington, *Letters written by Ebenezer Huntington during the American Revolution* (New York, 1915), 109.

57. Ebenezer Huntington to General Sullivan, "Sullivan Papers," *Collections of the New Hampshire Historical Society* (Concord, 1931), 14, 544.

58. Samuel B. Webb, Journal-1776, Samuel Blatchley Webb Papers.

59. General Washington to Brig. Gen. John Stark, February, 1780, quoted in Camus, *Military Music,* 312.

60. Ebenezer Huntington to Samuel B. Webb, February 16, 1780, in Webb, *Reminiscences,* 206.

61. Ebenezer Huntington to Samuel B. Webb, March, 1780, *Ibid.* 207.

62. *Record of Service,* 246.

63. *Ibid.,* 245.

64. Records of the First Congregational Church, East Hartford, 151. Olmstead published a collection of marches, *Martial Music* (Albany, 1807), in which "Col. Webb's Slow March" appears (No. 29).

65. Ebenezer Huntington to Samuel B. Webb, February 15, 1782, in *Family Letters of Samuel Blatchley Webb 1764-1807,* ed. W. C. Ford (New York, 1912), 184-85.

66. *Record of Service,* 250.

67. *Ibid.,* 148.

68. *Connecticut Courant,* March 14, 1780.

69. *Ibid.,* July 22, 1776.

70. Andrew Law, *Select Harmony* (Cheshire, 1778), title page.

71. New London *Connecticut Gazette,* July 10, 1778.

72. Calbraith B. Perry, *Charles D'Wolf of Guadaloupe, his Ancestors and Descendants* (New York, 1902), 122.

73. Richard Crawford, "Massachusetts Musicians and the Core Repertory of Early American Psalmody," *Music in Colonial Massachusetts.* A comprehensive index of the American fuging tune repertory, to be published by Detroit Information Coordinators, Inc., is in preparation at the University of Illinois, by Nicholas Temperley and Carl Manns.

74. Crawford, *Law*, 32.

75. *Ibid.*, 35.

76. Irving Lowens, "Andrew Law and the Pirates," *Music and Musicians in Early America* (New York, 1964), 60. See, in addition, "Copyright and Andrew Law," *Papers of the Bibliographical Society of America*, LIII (1959), 158-59.

77. Stiles, *Diary*, II, 400.

78. David Warren Steel, "Truman S. Wetmore (1774-1861): Connecticut Psalmodist" (MA Thesis, University of Michigan, 1976), 15.

79. Records of East Windsor Society, in Stiles, *Windsor*, I, 730.

80. Benjamin Trumbull, transcripts of North Haven Church records, Misc. Letters and Papers, North Haven Mss., Beinecke Rare Book and Manuscript Library, Yale University, New Haven.

81. *Ibid.*

82. Benjamin Trumbull, Psalm Tunes, original and selected, Z 36.283, Beinecke Rare Book and Manuscript Library, Yale University, New Haven. The music is from the contemporary British-American repertory.

83. Trumbull, transcripts, Misc. Letters and Papers, Beinecke Rare Book and Manuscript Library.

84. *Ibid.*

85. *Ibid.*

86. Baldwin, *Life and Letters*, 56.

87. *Ibid.*, 5.

88. Abbé Robin, *New Travels through North America* (Philadelphia, 1783), 24.

89. Meyer, *Congregationalism*, facsimile of "Independence," 32-33.

90. Webb, *Reminiscences*, 318.

91. Rabson, *Songbook*, 27.

92. Worthington Ford, *Broadsides, Ballads &c. Printed in Massachusetts, 1639-1800* (Boston, 1922), 294.

93. Broadside, Research Library, Old Sturbridge Village, Sturbridge, Massachusetts.

94. Oscar G. Sonneck published his findings, *sans* source location for the tune, in *"Report on 'The Star-Spangled Banner,' 'Hail Columbia,' 'America,' 'Yankee Doodle'"* (Washington, 1909). His work has not been superceded.

95. *Boston Journal*, September 29, 1768.

96. Trumbull, *M'Fingal*, Canto First, 3; Canto Second, 33.

97. Broadside, Philip H. and A.S.W. Rosenbach Foundation, reproduced in Lawrence, *Music*, 61.

98. James Halliwell, *Nursery Rhymes of England* (London, 1842), 82.

99. Summary in Kate Keller, "Yankee Doodle Riding a Phony?", *Hartford Courant*, February 19, 1978.

100. *Connecticut Courant*, January 8, 1782. An inventory of political and patriotic lyrics in colonial newspapers, including Connecticut's, from 1773 to 1783, is Gillian Anderson's *Freedom's Voice in Poetry and Song* (Wilmington, 1977).

101. Camus, *Military Music*, 163-65.

102. Brown, who served with the Fourth Connecticut Regiment, was from Durham. His fife manuscript was recently found by Kate Keller in the Daniel Read Collection, Box V, Folder G, at the New Haven Colony Historical Society, New Haven.

103. The libretto was printed in the *Norwich Packet*, February 28, 1782.

CHAPTER IV

1. The *New-Haven Gazette, and the Connecticut Magazine,* February 1, 1787.

2. *The American Magazine* (June 1788), 448. An editorial "On Psalmody," in the *Norwich Packet,* November 20, 1789, concluded that "As music produces much good on the moral faculties: so also it materially affects the health of the body. It has been often observed that those who sing much are seldom or never troubled with inward weakness: The exercise which it affords to the lungs prevents any consumptive disorders from being seated there."

3. Stiles, *Diary,* III, 277.

4. William Bentley, *The Diary of William Bentley, D.D. Pastor of East Church, Salem, Massachusetts* (Salem: Essex Institute, 1905-1914), II, 246, quoted in Richard Crawford, "Connecticut Sacred Music Imprints, 1778-1810," *Music Library Association Notes,* 27 (1971), 445. Crawford has completed a Bibliography of Sacred Music Published in America through 1810, to be published by the American Antiquarian Society, Worcester, Massachusetts.

5. The *Norwich Packet,* February 14, 1782.

6. Simeon Jocelin and Amos Doolittle, *The Chorister's Companion* (New Haven, 1782), [13]. These directions are from John Arnold, whose *Compleat Psalmodist* recommends that "the first thing to be done in the vocal Performance is to have your Voice as clear as possible, and to give every Note a clear and distinct sound; neither forcing the Sound through your Nose, nor blowing your Breath through your Teeth with your Mouth shut (which is the fault of several) and is offensive to a Musical Ear whenever they sing alone . . ." (Of Tuning the Voice; . . .)

7. *The Connecticut Journal,* March 14, 1782.

8. *Ibid.,* February 13, 1783.

9. *Ibid.,* November 21, 1782.

10. *Connecticut Courant,* January 8, 1782.

11. Jocelin and Doolittle, *Companion,* Preface, [1].

12. *Ibid.,* 60.

13. Sherman W. Adams and Henry R. Stiles, *The History of Ancient Wethersfield* (2 Vols., New York, 1974 reprint), I, 799.

14. Larned, *Windham,* I, 369.

15. *Ibid.*

16. Francisco de Miranda, *The Diary of Francisco de Miranda . . . 1783-84,* ed. William S. Robertson (New York, 1928), 80-81. Translation prepared by Dr. Sue Matz Soterakos, Southern Connecticut State College.

17. Oliver Brownson, *Select Harmony* (1783), Preface.

18. *Connecticut Courant,* March 15, 1785.

19. See Sterling E. Murray, "Timothy Swan and Yankee Psalmody," *The Musical Quarterly,* LXI (1975), 439.

20. Crawford, *Law,* 63, 75.

21. Frank J. Metcalf, *American Writers and Compilers of Sacred Music* (New York, 1925), 90-93. According to Metcalf (and George Hood in *History of Music in New England* [Boston, 1846]), Benham was born in 1757, but the Barbour file at The Connecticut State Library lists an Asahel Benham, born December 15, 1754, to Samuell and Phebe, in New Hartford. Benham died before, rather than in, 1805; his inventory was recorded December 14, 1803, in the Wallingford Probate Records.

22. Brownson, *Select Harmony,* 65, reproduced with permission of The Connecticut Historical Society, Hartford.

23. CM is Common Meter, or Ballad Meter (8.6.8.6.); SM is Short Meter (6.6.8.6.); LM is Long Meter (8.8.8.8); and PM is Particular Meter.

24. *Connecticut Courant,* January 23, 1786.

25. Emily Cordelia Swan, Notes, 1, Swan Papers, American Antiquarian Society, Worcester, Massachusetts.

26. *Connecticut Courant,* November 28, 1785.

27. E. Webster, Timothy Swan (Memoir), August 1842, Swan Papers.

28. *Ibid.*

29. Timothy Swan, Single sheet containing music and poem, Swan Papers.

30. Timothy Swan, Ms. Tune Book for violin, Swan Papers. The Connecticut Historical Society possesses another early music manuscript written by Swan, a small notebook containing rules of music, possibly a teaching aid. See Guy B. Webb, "Timothy Swan, Yankee Tunesmith" (D.M.A. thesis, University of Illinois, 1972), 12-13.

31. Alan Buechner, *The New England Harmony, Notes with Folkways FA* 2377 (New York, 1964), 21.

32. See Vinson C. Bushnell, "Daniel Read of New Haven (1757-1836): The Man and his Musical Activities" (Ph.D. dissertation, Harvard University, 1978).

33. A copy in Read's hand is in his Letterbook, at New Haven Colony Historical Society, and quoted in Buechner, "Singing Schools," 142.

34. Britton, "Theoretical Introductions," 647.

35. Lowens, *Music and Musicians,* 159-60.

36. Thaddeus Larned (1786) and Simon Larned (1783), Commonplace book (music), Hartford Seminary Foundation Archives, Hartford.

37. Advertising Supplement, *The New-Haven Gazette, and Connecticut Magazine,* March 23, 1786. A facsimile edition edited by Annemarie Schnase was published in Scarsdale, New York in 1961.

38. *Ibid.*

39. *The Connecticut Journal,* March 29, 1786.

40. Britton, "Theoretical Introductions," 536.

41. Carpenter was born in Rehoboth on December 18, 1752, to Eleazer and Elizabeth Carpenter, according to James N. Arnold, *Vital Record of Rehoboth; 1642-1896* (2 Vols., Providence, 1897), II, 130. Carpenter and Read may have been related, since there are many relations between the two families.

42. The title page carries the inscription "Elihu Carpenter of Rehoboth his Book given him by the authors. May 13, 1783." This copy is at Beinecke Rare Book and Manuscript Library, Yale University, New Haven.

43. See Crawford, *Law,* Chapter III, "The Itinerant Singing Master (1783-92)," 36-85.

44. *Ibid.,* 34.

45. Ford, *Life of Noah Webster,* I, 151, entry March 11, 1786.

46. Warfel, *Noah Webster,* 20.

47. Records of the First Ecclesiastical Society, West Hartford.

48. Ford, *Life of Noah Webster,* I, 80-81, 84, entries of October 8, and August 10, 1784.

49. *Ibid.,* I, 80, 82, 132, 135. Simeon Baldwin mentioned going to Dr. Smith's in Albany, after tea, and spending "the remainder of the afternoon in singing of Psalm tunes, according to the custom of New England." (*Life and Letters,* Journal entry for the Sabbath, April 27, 1783.)

50. Advertisement dated May 25, 1785, quoted in Warfel, *Noah Webster,* 124.

51. Ford, *Life of Noah Webster*, I, 139-140.

52. Warfel, *Noah Webster*, 124-25.

53. Records of the First Church of Christ, New Haven, 180; Records of Newington Society quoted in Adams and Stiles, *Ancient Wethersfield*, I, 799.

54. Records of Hartford First Society, quoted in Buechner, "Yankee Singing Schools," 192.

55. Before the war, Colonel John Benjamin had served as organist (1757-76) without compensation. The church did pay Thomas Stratton 2s. from the Communion collection "to mend upon the Organ" in 1763. Organists after the war were: Captain George Benjamin—1780 (Col. John's brother or nephew); Philip Benjamin-1780-83 (brother), Asa Benjamin—1783-89 (son); and William Benjamin—chosen April 13, 1789 (son). Information in Stratford, Minutes and Registers, I, and Ruth Wilson, "Christ Church, Stratford: A Case History," unpublished paper.

56. Stiles, *Diary*, III, 201.

57. G. Huntington Byles, *A Short History of The Organs and Music of Trinity Church, New Haven, Connecticut* (New Haven: Prepared for the 200th Anniversary of Trinity Church, 1752-1952), 15. The Holland organ, purchased by subscription, was repaired and enlarged by the firm of William Redstone, New York, in 1815, and served until 1844.

58, The *Norwich Packet*, September 26, 1782. At Phillips Exeter Academy in neighboring Massachusetts, preceptor Eliphalet Pearson devoted afternoon hours to students singing instruction and was responsible for "examining & correcting, note by note, all their musical manuscripts." (Memorial to the Trustees, April 17, 1780, Park Family Papers, Mss. and Archives, Yale University Library, New Haven.)

59. Stiles, *Diary*, III, 322, entry from the College Memoranda.

60. Baldwin, *Life and Letters*, 187. The agreement to form the school was signed by eighteen members of the sophomore class.

61. Stiles, *Diary*, II, 554.

62. *Ibid.*, III, 102.

63. *Ibid.*

64. *Ibid.*, III, 201.

65. *Ibid.*, 184. Yale commencements were not all "solemnities." Count dal Verme, who received an honorary degree in September 1784, noted: "Some persons were on the bell tower blowing little trumpets. After fireworks and many rockets [in the evening], every room of any size was converted into a ball room; a violin in one, a small trumpet in another, and even a lone drum in another sufficed to set in motion the legs of these people so passionately fond of dancing." (*The Journals and Letters of Count Francisco dal Verme-1783-84*, trans. and ed. Elizabeth Cometti, Charlottesville, 1969, 27.)

66. Smith's advertisement in *The Connecticut Journal*, July 4, 1782. Beers' notice in *The New-Haven Gazette and Connecticut Magazine*, Advertising Supplement, December 29, 1785. Beers was the parish clerk at Trinity Church in 1785. (Frederick Croswell, "History of Trinity Church, New Haven," *Papers of the New Haven Colony Historical Society*, I, 76.)

67. Stiles, *Diary*, III, 236.

68. The *New-Haven Gazette, and Connecticut Magazine*, March 16, 1786.

69. *Ibid.*, February 16, 1786, Advertising Supplement No. 1.

70. [Chauncey Langdon], *The Beauties of Psalmody* (New Haven, 1786), Preface.

71. The *New-Haven Gazette and Connecticut Magazine*, Advertising Supplement, May 11, 1786.

72. [Chauncey Langdon], *The Select Songster* (New Haven, 1786), Preface. The usual definition of a songster is a collection of lyrics without notation, as used in Irving Lowens' *A Bibliography of Songsters Printed in America Before 1821* (Worcester, 1976). Langdon produced an eighteenth-century work of musical scholarship of sorts by "procuring the Notes" of tunes from oral tradition.

73. Simeon Jocelin, *A Collection of Favorite Psalm Tunes, From late and approved British Authors* (New Haven, 1787). This work of sixteen pages, on the scale of the *Chorister's Companion*, was advertised to contain all pieces "never before printed in America" and sold for 1s. 6d. *Connecticut Courant*, March 19, 1787.

74. "The British Muse" is the melody of the final chorus in Act III of the opera. Another tune with a second part added in *Select Songster* is "Fare well ye greenfields," printed as a song and an instrumental piece in a number of British collections. With a text adapted for the purpose, the tune was taken into the repertory of southern fasola singers. George P. Jackson lists the tune, No. 72, in his eighty most popular tunes in *White Spirituals in the Southern Uplands* (New York, Dover reprint, 1965), 148.

75. The *American Mercury*, July 28, 1788.

76. *Ibid.*, November 3, 1788.

77. *Ibid.*, January 19, 1789. The performance was advertised as well in the *Connecticut Courant*, under the same date. See Kenneth Silverman, *A Cultural History of the American Revolution* (New York, 1976), 558-63, for a discussion of *The Contrast*.

78. The *Norwich Packet*, May 29, 1789. The other seven verses of the song laud the virtues of commerce and manufactures as avenues to wealth and prosperity.

For Further Reading

General music histories contain only sketchy information about Connecticut music and musicians; the most useful general works and bibliographical tools are cited in the NOTES. There are basic articles: Nathan H. Allen's "Old Time Music and Musicians" (*Connecticut Magazine*, 1895) and Richard Crawford's "Connecticut Sacred Music Imprints, 1778-1810" (Music Library Association *Notes*, 27, 1971). Allen's unpublished book-length manuscript on general Connecticut music history can be read at Watkinson Library at Trinity College in Hartford. It contains several chapters on the period before 1800 and discusses psalmody and some secular music, especially the Hartford theater scene in the 1790s.

There are a few specialized works dealing with music in Connecticut before 1800, particularly those about some of the major eighteenth-century composer/compilers. Richard Crawford's biography of Andrew Law, Irving Lowens' articles on Daniel Read and Andrew Law (in *Music and Musicians in Early America*), Vinson C. Bushnell's Harvard doctoral dissertation on Daniel Read, Sterling Murray's *Musical Quarterly* article and University of Michigan Master's thesis on Timothy Swan, and Guy Webb's Illinois doctoral thesis on Timothy Swan are cited in full in the NOTES. David Warren Steel's Michigan Master's thesis on Truman Wetmore contains useful information, although Wetmore was active professionally in the early nineteenth century. Steel is also at work on a doctoral dissertation on Stephen Jenks.

Some early music is now available in modern editions, and a few Connecticut composers are represented in *Music in America*, an anthology of music from 1620-1865, by W. Thomas Marocco and Harold Gleason, published by Norton (1964). *Giles Gibbs, His Book for the Fife*, edited by Kate V.W. Keller (1974), is available from The Connecticut Historical Society. Country dance music figures have been published in two collections: Keller and Sweet, *A Choice Selection of American Country Dances of the Revolutionary Era* (1976), and James Morrison's *Twenty-Four Early American Country Dances* (1976). A number of good recordings contain military and popular music; two recordings recommended for their selection and performance style are Arthur F. Schrader's *American Revolutionary War Songs* (Folkways FH 5279) and *The New England Harmony* (Folkways FA 2377), prepared at Old Sturbridge Village in Massachusetts under Schrader's direction.

Index

Prepared by Kate Van Winkle Keller

Including contemporary names, titles of books and theater works, titles and first lines of musical works, and subjects discussed.

Grounds and Rules of Musick. See
Walter, Thomas

"Hail the day, that sees him rise," 88
Hale, Nathan, 51
Hale, Samuel, 71
Hamelton, Thomas, 67
Handel, George Frederick, 66, 76, 107,
109, 111; "Air by Handel," 76, 77;
Atalanta, 111; "Minuet by Handel,"
76; *Occasional Oratorio*, 74; "Water
Piece," 109
Hanks, Benjamin, 71, 76
Hanks, Uriah, 76
"Hanover, thou land of pleasure," 49
"Hark from the tombs a doleful sound,"
78
Harland, Thomas, 76
Harrington, Henry, 51
Harrison, Joseph, 47
Hart, Deacon, 22
Hartford Wits, 48
Harvard College, 25, 47, 113
Hawley, Joseph, 22
"Hearts of Oak," 43-44
Hempstead, Joshua, 36
Hibbard, David, Jr., 71
Hill, Belah, 89
Hill, John, 89
Hillhouse, James, 51
Hitchcock, Mr., 108
Hiwell, John, 82
Holland, Henry, 108
Hollister, David, 71
"Holy holy holy Lord God almighty,"
101
"Honour of a London Prentice, The,"
67
Hook, James, 103
Hooker, William, 84-86
Hopkinson, Francis, 94
Horton, Nathaniel, 18
Hosmer, Prosper, 84-86
Hosmer, Thomas, 17-18
How, Ephraim, 33
Howlet, William, 71
Hubbard, Bela, 89
Hulett, William C., 39
Humphreys, David (?), 108
Huntington, Caleb, 87
Huntington, Ebenezer, 70, 84, 86
"Hymn on the Divine Use of Musick,"
103

"Hymn on the Vanity of the World,"
103
hymns, 13, 27-30, 37-38, 42-43, 61, 64
Hymns and Spiritual Songs. See Watts,
Isaac

"In good King Charles' golden days,"
45
"In sixteen hundred sixty-two," 45
"Independence," 92
Indian music, 123
"Indian Philosopher, The," 103
Indians, musical education of, 60-62,
117-18n67
Ingersol, Mr., 55
instruction and instructors: dancing, 32,
39; instrumental, 52, 83, 86; methods,
25, 40, 56-59, 97, 109; singing, 9,
15, 18, 22, 24-25, 41, 51-62, 80, 87-
91, 95-100, 103, 106-108, 13n58. *See
also* majors, drum and fife; self-
instruction and tutors
instruments, musical, 32-36, 39, 48, 52,
66, 82-84, 86, 89, 108, 109. *See also*
drums, fifes, flutes, french horns, jews
harps, organs, pitch-pipes, trumpets,
violins
*Introduction to the Art of Singing Psalm
Tunes. See Very Plain and Easy Introduction. . .*

Jenks, Stephen, 133
Jennings, Jonathan, Jr., 71
jews harps, 31, 119n101
Jocelin, Simeon, 96-98, 100, 106, 111;
Chorister's Companion, 96-98, 104,
106, 109, 111; *Collection of Favorite
Psalm Tunes*, 111
Johnson, Joseph, 61, 80
Johnson, Mr., 50
Johnson, William Samuel, 32
Jones, Epraphas, 84-86
Jones, Thomas, 87
"Judgment," 106

Keen, Robert, 60
Kellogg, Jacob, 18
Kimberly, Nathaniel, 33
Kimberly, Thos., 33
King, Charles, Jr., 71
King, Oliver, 54, 55, 88
"King George's March," 126n24
Kirkland, Samuel, 61

107, 130n49; printed, owned by Connecticut residents, 12, 15, 24-26, 28-29, 40-41, 61, 76, 106; printed, sold in Connecticut, 40-42, 56-59, 82-83, 109; published in Connecticut, 56-60, 87-89, 96-106, 109-11; "sacred" and "secular," lack of clear distinction between, 103; theoretical dissertations, 25-26; 56, 90; value of, personal and social, 13-14, 27, 29, 61, 95-96, 107, 129n2

Musical Entertainer (Bickham), 28

Musical Miscellany (Watts), 28, 40-41

New Version of the Psalms of David. *See* Brady, Nicholas

"Newbury," 90

"New-England, raise thy grateful voice," 37

Niles, Nathaniel, 70

Nye, David, 71

"O nightingale best poet of the grove," 102

"O praise the Lord, O my soul," 100

"O the dessolation of Sion," 27

Occasional Oratorio (Handel), 74

Occum, Sampson, 60, 61; *Collection of Hymns and Spiritual Songs,* 60, 87

"Ode for Christmas," 106

"Ode on Spring," 103

old-way singing, 10, 19-21. *See also* church music

Olmstead, Timothy, 71, 76, 84-86

"On Musick," 100

organs and organists, 11, 32, 52, 108, 131n55

Otis, James, 121n23

"Over the Hills and Far Away," 74

"Over the Water to Charly," 77

Paine, Elisha, 29

Paine, Phillip, 55

Pall, John, 71

Parks, Frederick, 86

Parmele, Abel, 36

part-books, manuscript, 56-58

Patten, Nathaniel, 58, 87

payment of musicians. *See* salaries

Payson, Jonathan, 17

"Pax Tune," 22

Peake, Goodman, 36

Pearson, Eliphalet, 131n58

Pease, Aaron, 71

Pease, Calvin, 76, 78, 80

pedlars, 40, 67

Perry, John, 16

Pese, Isack, 18

Peters, Samuel, 7, 119n101

Pickering, Timothy, 96

Pickett, Goodman, 36

Pinney, Lemuel, 71

pitch-pipe, 89, 109

Pixley, Mr., 51

Platt, Jeremiah, 32

Playford, Henry, *Divine Companion,* 28

Playford, John: *English Dancing Master,* 31; *Introduction to the Skill of Musick,* 15, 28; *Whole Book of Psalms,* 28

"Plymouth," 90

"Poland," 100

Pomeroy, Benjamin, 78

"Pompey's Ghost," 56, 103

Porter, Samuel, 34-35

Porter, William, 34-35

precentor, 16

professionalism in music, 116n31

"Prospect of the Future Glory of America" (Trumbull), 48

psalms: setting of, by leader, 16-19, 22, 60; settings, musical: "Psalm 34," 90; "Psalm 46," 90; "Psalm 73," 105; "Psalm 108," 57; "Psalm 115;" 90; "Psalm 122," 90; "Psalm 136," 88; "Psalm 149," 76; "Psalm Tune," 76; singing of. *See* church music; music, informal and domestic

Psalms of David Imitated. See Watts, Isaac

Puritans, attitude toward music, 7, 12-14, 27, 30

Putnam, Israel, 72, 92

"Queane Nab," 79

"Rainbow," 100

"Rakes of Mallow," 31

"Rakes of Marlow Quick Time," 32

"Rapture, The," 77

Read, Daniel, 96, 97, 100, 103-105, 106, 111, 133; *American Singing Book,* 96, 100, 103-04, 09.

teachers of music. *See* instruction and instructors; majors, drum and fife

"Thanksgiving Hymn, A," 37

"That seat of science Athens," 125n113

theater. *See* dramatic performances

"Thehos Gendar," 92

Thompson, Aaron, 78, 81, 86, 126n23

"Thy praise alone, O Lord, doth reign," 27

"Thy word the raging wind control," 98

Tibbals, Thomas (?), 74

"Tipling Philosopher, The," 47

"To Arms," 73

Todd, Ebenezer, 90

Todd, Ithamar, 90

Todd, Jesse, 90

Todd, Jonathan, 32

Treat, Jonathan, 71

Trumbull, Benjamin, 47, 56, 64-65, 83, 89-91, 103, 123n70

Trumbull, David (?), 44-45

Trumbull, John, 48, 80, 93; *M'Fingal,* 80, 82, 93

Trumbull, John (printer), 114

Trumbull, Martha Phelps (Mrs. Benjamin), 91

trumpets and trumpeters, 34, 36, 65-66, 71-72, 82, 119n101, 131n65

Tryon, William, 71

Tufts, John, 24, 25; *Very Plain and Easy Introduction to the Singing of Psalm Tunes,* 24-26, 28

Tuttle, Solomon, 90

" 'Twas winter and blue Tory noses were freezing," 92

Tyler, Nathaniel, 71

Tyler, Royall, *The Contrast,* 113

Universal Psalmodist. See Williams, Aaron

Urania. See Lyon, James

usual-way singing, 9-24. *See also* church music

Very Plain and Easy Introduction . . . See Tufts, John

"Vicar of Bray," 44-45

"Virginia," 98

violin and violists, 32, 39, 47-48, 52, 66, 82-83, 102, 109, 110, 131n65

Virgin Unmask'd or An Old Man taught Wisdom, 113

Von Steuben, Baron, 82

Wadsworth, Daniel, 30

Wadsworth, Lieutenant, 78

"Wakefield," 100

Waldo, Cornelius, 71

Wales, Samuel, 11-12, 104

Walter, Thomas, 24, 25; *Grounds and Rules of Musick,* 24-26, 28, 41

"Wantage," 90

Warner, Stephen, 71

Washburn, Moses, 71

"Washington," 108

Washington, George, 72, 73, 85, 92, 94, 96

"Water Piece," (Handel), 109

Watson, John, Jr., 71

Watts, Isaac, 27-29, 60, 78; *Divine Songs for Children,* 28-29, 41; *Horae Lyricae,* 28; *Hymns and Spiritual Songs,* 28-29, 40, 41, 64, 87; *Psalms of David,* 15, 28-29, 40, 41, 87, 89

Webb, Charles B., 86

Webb, Joseph, 99

Webb, Samuel B., 48, 70, 82, 83, 84, 85, 92

Webster, Abraham, 106

Webster, Daniell, 17-18

Webster, Noah, 70, 72, 95, 106, 107

Webster, Noah, Sr., 106

"Welcome Song," 103

"Welcome welcome ev'ry guest," frontispiece

Wesley, John, 60

West, Benjamin, 103

Wetmore, Truman, 133

Wheelock, Eleazer, 29, 60, 78

"While I relate my story," 92

Whipple, Noah, 71

Whitaker, Nathaniel, 60

White, Peregrine, 76

Whitear, John, 36

Whitefield, George, 60

Whiting, Charles, 83

Whiting, Nathan, 65

Whiting, Samuel, 56

Whitman, John, 107

Whitman, Rev., 30

Whitman, Samuel, 56, 58, 103, 107, 123n70

Whitmore, Jacob, 53

"Who has e'er been at Versailles," 49

"Who has e'er been at Balldock," 49